insight text guide

Ruth Thomas

Stasiland

Anna Funder

First published in 2012, reprinted in 2013, 2014, 2015, 2016 (three times), 2017, 2019, 2020, 2021.

Insight Publications Pty Ltd
3/350 Charman Road
Cheltenham VIC 3192
Australia
Tel: +61 3 8571 4950
Fax: +61 3 8571 0257
Email: books@insightpublications.com.au

www.insightpublications.com.au

National Library of Australia Cataloguing-in-Publication entry:
Thomas, Ruth, 1980–
Anna Funder's stasiland / Ruth Thomas.
9781922004031 (pbk.)
Insight text guide.
Includes bibliographical references.
For secondary school age.
Funder, Anna, 1966—Stasiland.
Funder, Anna, 1966—Criticism and interpretation.
943.10870922

Other ISBNs:
9781925175172 (digital)
9781925175509 (bundle: print + digital)

Cover design: The Modern Art Production Group

Printed by Markono Print Media Pte Ltd

contents

CHARACTER MAP

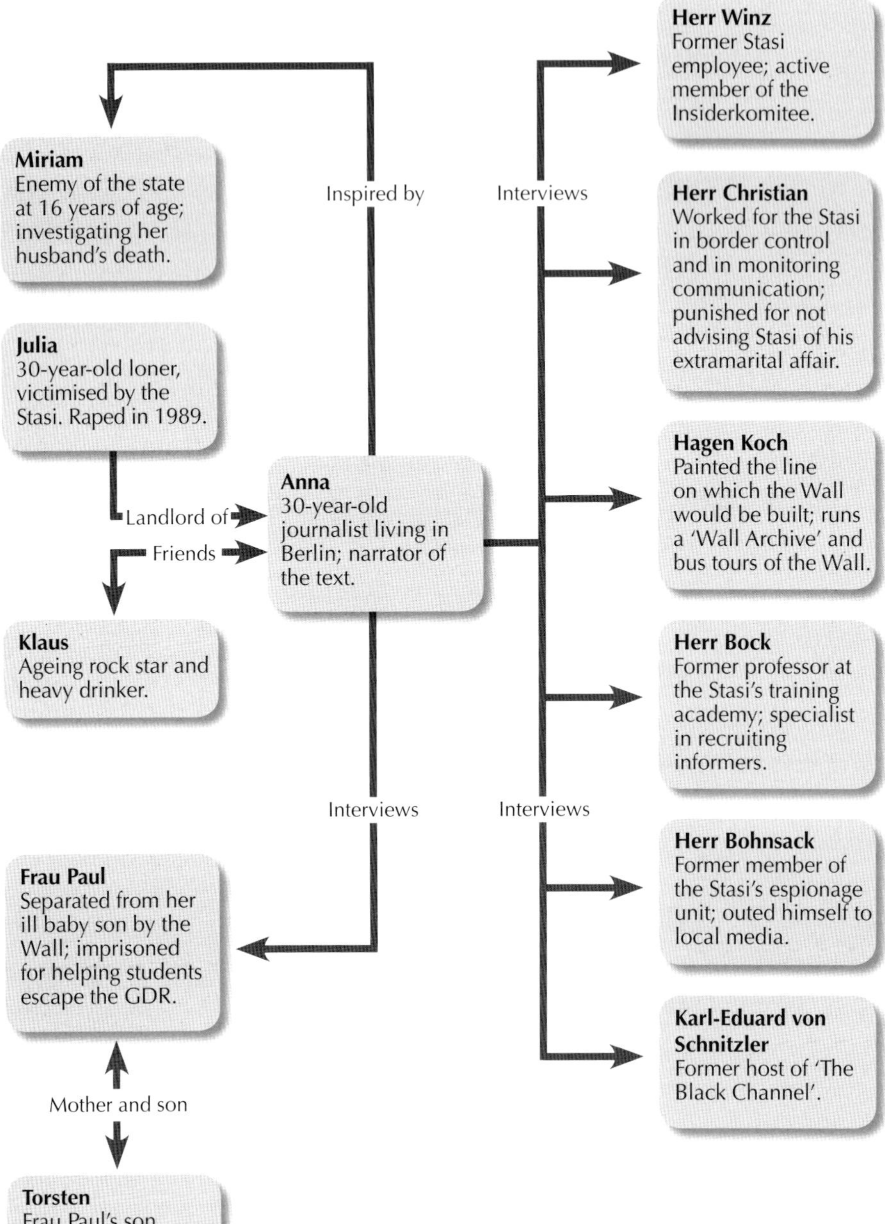

OVERVIEW

About the author

Anna Funder is an acclaimed Australian writer. Born in 1966, she grew up in Melbourne and Paris, and lived in West Berlin as a university student in the 1980s. It was on this trip that she first began to wonder about life behind the Berlin Wall, a fascination that years later would result in her first book, *Stasiland* (2002). After her studies in Arts and Law, Funder worked as an international lawyer for the Australian Government, specialising in constitutional law, human rights and treaty negotiation. In the mid-1990s she abandoned law to write. She published articles and essays in a range of Australian newspapers and serials including the *Sydney Morning Herald*, *The Monthly* and *Best Australian Essays*.

Funder attained critical acclaim with the publication of *Stasiland*: it was awarded the 2004 BBC Four Samuel Johnson Prize, the most prestigious prize for nonfiction writing in the United Kingdom. *Stasiland* was also nominated for the *Guardian* first book award (UK) and *The Age* Book of the Year and Queensland Premier's Literary awards in Australia. It has since been published in sixteen languages in some twenty countries and features in school and university courses in both Australia and the UK.

Funder's second book, the novel *All That I Am* (2011) explores similar themes and settings to *Stasiland*. Based on real people and real events, *All That I Am* describes the life in exile of a group of writers, journalists and agitators who flee the growing danger and madness in Nazi Germany and seek refuge in London. Set in the 1930s when Nazism was beginning to take hold in Germany, *All That I Am* celebrates courage and moral strength in the face of fear and tyranny, just as *Stasiland* does for a different generation of German people.

Both *Stasiland* and *All That I Am* were inspired by Funder's real-life friendship with a central character. *Stasiland* is crafted around Funder's attempt to tell the story of Miriam Weber, a woman she befriended in

Leipzig in the late 1990s. In *All That I Am* Funder similarly reconstructs the life of her friend Ruth Blatt. *All That I Am* has brought Funder further accolades and recognition. This work has been awarded numerous literary prizes, including Australia's highest honour for fiction writing, the Miles Franklin Prize, as well as the Indie Book of the Year, the ABIA Book of the Year and the Barbara Jefferis awards.

Synopsis

Stasiland is a collection of personal stories that reveals what life was like for ordinary people living behind the Berlin Wall. These stories are collated by Anna – visitor, interviewer and narrator – who gives voice both to victims and to people who worked for the Stasi, East Germany's infamous secret service. (*Stasiland* is an example of literary journalism written in the first person. It is helpful to distinguish between Funder the author of the text, and Anna the narrative voice and a central character in the text. In the same way, the people Funder writes about can be understood as characters, in the sense that they are deliberately constructed by the author, as well as being real, living individuals.) After two visits to Germany – one in the 1980s when the Wall still hid the realities of the East German regime and another in 1994 when the recently unified Germany was uncovering and sharing those secrets – Anna is intrigued. She is particularly fascinated by the story of Miriam Weber, whose husband died in Stasi custody. In 1996, Anna returns to Berlin, secures work at a local television station and begins her investigation of life in the GDR.

Anna's first interview is with Miriam. Miriam recounts how she became an enemy of the state at sixteen after she printed and distributed pamphlets criticising the police's harsh treatment of protestors in Leipzig. While awaiting trial, Miriam attempts to escape over the Berlin Wall on New Year's Eve, 1968. Again she is arrested and interrogated. This time she is subjected to illegal sleep deprivation then incarcerated for eighteen months in a brutal women's prison. After her release she marries Charlie, a young man also under the Stasi's careful watch. Charlie later dies in a prison cell.

Anna seeks out other stories to help her understand Miriam's. She places an advertisement in the personals column of her local paper, seeking former Stasi employees – official and unofficial – for interview. Five men respond: Herr Winz, who reveals that the dangers of the Stasi continue in the activities of the *Insiderkomitee*; Herr Christian, who recalls his time working for the Stasi's border control operations as an amusing game; Herr Koch, who, as a Stasi recruit, painted the line that marked where the Wall would be built; Herr Bock, who trained recruits at the Ministry's academy; and Herr Bohnsack, who worked as an overseas spy. Anna also interviews Karl-Eduard von Schnitzler, who wrote and presented 'The Black Channel' on East German television for nearly thirty years. Anna's visits to key Stasi locations – first the national Stasi headquarters at Normannenstrasse, then the East German television station and Hohenschönhausen prison – provide her with opportunities to ruminate on the things she has learned, to collect evidence and to see the instruments of Stasi power first-hand. Interspersed with the stories told by those on the inside are the stories told by the victims. These include Anna's friends Julia and Klaus, as well as Sigrid Paul, whom Anna seeks out on the advice of a tour guide at Stasi headquarters.

On the night of her last interview, Anna receives an urgent phone call from Australia. She returns immediately and, in the wake of her mother's death, puts her project on hiatus until she can return to Berlin in the spring of 2000. On her return, she re-establishes contact with Julia, who has since moved to a promising new life in San Francisco, and with Hagen Koch, who capitalises on his unique knowledge of the Wall by driving tour buses around its ruins. Anna also finally visits the 'puzzlers', employees of the Stasi File Authority who reconstruct Stasi files largely destroyed during the regime's last days from the scraps that remain, on whom Miriam has pinned hope of an explanation regarding Charlie's death. Distraught at the unlikelihood of such a discovery, Anna visits Miriam a second time. In this meeting, Miriam speaks more openly about Charlie and her own ideas about what happened. Her preparedness to share stories, photos and poems with Anna shows that she has made peace with her past, enabling the text to close with a sense of hope, largely absent in the bleak stories and settings that lead up to this point.

Character summaries

Anna: An Australian living temporarily in Berlin, thirty-year-old Anna is the text's narrator.

Miriam Weber: Aged in her mid-forties, Miriam has spent much of her life fighting the Stasi. She became an enemy of the state at sixteen years of age. She almost escaped East Berlin in 1968, but was caught, tried and imprisoned. After her release she married Charlie, who later died in Stasi custody. She has spent decades seeking answers.

Julia Behrend: Julia is Anna's landlord. The Stasi closely monitored Julia because of her relationship with an Italian man. The Stasi also covertly controlled her education and employment. Julia was raped just after the Wall fell. She is mistrustful, anxious and unable to submit to authority. She moves to San Francisco to start a new life.

Frau Sigrid Paul: Frau Paul is in her early sixties. She volunteers at the museum set up in the former Hohenschönhausen prison, where she was incarcerated in the 1960s for helping students escape East Berlin. She refused a Stasi deal to inform on a friend and, in so doing, relinquished all opportunity of seeing her infant son, who was in a West Berlin hospital.

Torsten: Frau Paul's son. Born with life-threatening injuries, Torsten spent his first five years in a West Berlin hospital. Anna meets Torsten as an adult.

Klaus Renft: A founding member of the Klaus Renft Combo, one of East Germany's most popular rock groups, which was banned by the Stasi in 1975. Klaus is easygoing, philosophical and a heavy drinker.

Alexander Scheller: Anna's boss at West Berlin's overseas television station. His dismissive attitude toward East Germans strengthens Anna's determination to research and write Miriam's story.

Uwe Schmidt: Anna's colleague who helps her track down von Schnitzler and Hagen Koch.

Karl-Eduard von Schnitzler: Von Schnitzler is seventy-nine years old and frail, but bullishly aggressive. Von Schnitzler researched, wrote and presented 'The Black Channel'. He remains staunchly committed to communist and GDR ideology.

Herr Winz: Herr Winz, in his sixties, still vehemently defends communism and is intent on putting forward the Stasi's side of history.

Herr Christian: Herr Christian worked in the Stasi's border control. He had no ideological commitment to the Stasi, but is a self-confessed stickler for the law.

Hagen Koch: Hagen Koch was employed in the Stasi's cartography department and in 1961 painted the line upon which the Berlin Wall was built. Now in his fifties, he preserves the Wall in his archive and in his work as a tour guide.

Herr Bock: Herr Bock was a professor at the Stasi's training academy where he taught Stasi men how to recruit informers. His quiet menace makes Anna uncomfortable.

Herr Bohnsack: Herr Bohnsack worked in the Stasi's overseas espionage department. He publicly admitted to being a Stasi man in a local bar in late 1989.

Herr Raillard: The director of the Stasi File Authority, Herr Raillard oversees the thirty-one 'puzzlers' attempting to reconstruct shredded Stasi files.

BACKGROUND & CONTEXT

A divided country

The Germany Anna visits in 1996 is a newly unified country, and one coming to terms with a painful and shameful history. Between 1945 and 1989 Germany was split into two distinct countries divided along geographical and ideological lines: capitalist West Germany (officially known as the Federal Republic of Germany or FDR) and communist East Germany (the German Democratic Republic or GDR). This tense situation was a direct outcome of the 1945 Potsdam Agreement (one of the treaties that officially ended World War II) in which the victorious Allies 'divided up their conquered enemy', Nazi Germany (p.160). England, the United States and France, united by their capitalist ethos and economies, gained control of Germany's western states. Communist Russia took control of the eastern states and established the GDR as a 'satellite state of the USSR' (p.161). Germany's capital Berlin was carved up between the victors in the same way: its western suburbs became the dominion of the English, United States and French governments, and its eastern ones became the territory of Soviet Russia. This created an untenable absurdity. Because Berlin was deep in the Soviet zone, its western suburbs 'became an odd island of democratic administration and market economy in a Communist landscape' (p.160).

The coexistence of two radically opposed politico-economic systems within the one city was virtually unmanageable. In the first decades after World War II, people travelled relatively freely across the divided city. West Germans could visit the eastern suburbs to buy the cheap eggs, milk, bread and meat that communist subsidies guaranteed for East Germans. East Germans could travel into West Berlin to work each day, taking advantage of the west's higher wages (p.170). Many East Berliners also used the open border for more permanent moves. By 1961, an estimated 2,000 people were defecting from East Germany each day, simply by travelling to Berlin's western suburbs and staying there (p.170). The friction this opportunistic border crisscrossing caused is expressed by Hagen Koch who, even in 1996, dubs West Germans who shopped in the east 'swindlers and parasites and black marketeers' and who is still furious with enterprising East Germans who worked for greater return in the west (p.170).

The localised tensions that Koch recalls were only part of the picture. On a world scale, escalating tension during the Cold War (the period of heightened tension between capitalist and communist countries from 1945 to 1990) meant that the permeable border between East and West Berlin became an embarrassment and a liability for the Communist Bloc (the communist states of Eastern Europe, including the GDR, Russia, Poland and the former Czechoslovakia). The solution was to build a wall: a fifty-two-kilometre construction of concrete, barbed wire, patrol strips and manned sentry towers.

Officially known as the 'anti-fascist protective measure' (p.171), the Wall was claimed by the East German government to be a necessary defence to protect East Germany's 17 million citizens from the tyranny and corruption of the west. This ideological rationalisation was not confined to the administration. Von Schnitzler's passionate justification of the Wall as 'humane' and 'the most useful construction' in Europe's history (p.134) illustrates the belief that die-hard communists had in the Wall. Even sceptics like Hagen Koch saw some value in it because it prevented people from shirking their responsibilities to the state that needed them, a position he claims to have been 'orthodox for the time' (p.170).

The Berlin Wall came to symbolise the deep divisions between eastern and western Europe during the Cold War. But for the people of Berlin, its impact was personal and tragic. Overnight, strings of barbed wire – the precursor to the concrete structure that would be built in the following weeks – appeared in the streets of Berlin's eastern zone. People woke on 13 August 1961 'to find themselves cut off from relatives, from work, from school' (p.171). The Wall 'was one of the longest structures ever built to keep people separate from one another' (p.3) – in this case, people of the one nation and often of the one family. The Wall separated Frau Paul from her gravely ill infant son, who was spirited across the border to a hospital in the western zone that could provide the specialist medicine he needed to survive. Michael Hinze, studying at a West Berlin university, was separated from his parents in Brandenburg (p.208). Men were shot and killed attempting to scale the Wall (p.125). Others caught attempting escape, like Miriam, were arrested, tried and incarcerated in psychologically damaging prisons. And the Wall kept secrets. Behind it, the Stasi – the GDR's 'internal army' (p.5) – perpetrated unimaginable horrors against its own citizens.

The Wall 'cut a strange wound through the city' (p.20), both physically and psychologically. Its significance, amplified in the text by Funder's deliberate capitalisation of the word 'wall', sits in contrast to its swift construction and equally rapid destruction. On 9 November 1989, after a series of radical changes in the Eastern Bloc and weeks of unrest in East Germany, the East German government announced that its citizens could freely visit the west. Jubilant crowds of East and West Germans climbed the Wall and began chipping away at the structure that had so defined and dictated their lives. By 1996, just six years after the formal reunification of Germany, Anna notes that there was 'hardly a trace of it in the streets' (p.172). In unified Germany, most people 'want to pretend it was never there' (p.172) or want to commemorate it in safe and sanitised ways, such as in museums, or through bus tours and souvenir stalls.

The Stasi

The Wall controlled travel; the Stasi controlled people. It prevented dissent, open debate and freedom of association and thereby kept the GDR's one-party democratic government in place from 1945 to 1989.

The Stasi, formally known as the Ministry for State Security, was the official security service of the GDR, a 'vast apparatus' commissioned with the task of knowing 'everything about everyone, using any means it chose' (p.5). It was founded on 8 February 1950 and was modelled on the USSR's Ministry for State Security. Under the command of Erich Mielke (Minister of State Security 1957–1989), the Stasi employed 97,000 full-time personnel (p.57). This personnel worked across the Ministry's two divisions: internal, known as 'Defence', and external, known as 'Counter-espionage'. As Herr Bock, a former professor at the Ministry's training academy, explains, the internal service was 'designed to spy on and control the citizens of the GDR' (p.196), while the external department had an international focus and worked to infiltrate foreign – particularly West German – political organisations. Two of the Stasi men interviewed in *Stasiland*, Herr Bock and Herr Bohnsack, worked for the Counter-espionage department. But Funder's main concern is in detailing the work, the power and the legacy of the internally focused Defence department.

The Stasi was so thorough, so meticulous and so innovative in its surveillance of East German citizens that it has become widely regarded as one of the world's most effective – and most repressive – secret police services. *Stasiland* is littered with examples of the organisation's extraordinary techniques. The exhibits Anna views at the museum in the former Stasi offices at Runde Ecke (p.7) – wigs and moustaches, microphones disguised as flowers, a list of silent signals for communicating information during covert observations – illustrate the level of deception involved in gathering information, and demonstrate the extent to which Stasi officers infiltrated the everyday lives of ordinary people. Citizens were subjected to constant scrutiny, and this was often so well disguised as to be virtually invisible. Stasi employees worked in prisons, in the police service and in administrative roles directly supporting the organisation's activities, but were also stationed as infiltrators in factories, church groups and schools to monitor the activities and actions of the GDR's citizens.

The work of official Stasi employees was supplemented by information supplied by an extensive network of informers or *inofizielle Mitarbeiter* (unofficial collaborators), ordinary people recruited by the Stasi to provide information about their own colleagues, friends and even families. An estimated 173,000 informers were recruited (p.57), either voluntarily because they believed in the cause, or as a result of coercion by the Stasi, in the way that Julia is pressured by Major N. (pp.111–12) and Frau Paul is manipulated by a lieutenant during a twenty-two-hour interrogation (p.219). Some 10,000 of the unofficial informers identified since the fall of the Wall were under eighteen years of age when recruited by the Stasi. Informants were offered social and financial incentives such as gifts, money and birthday presents. But as Herr Bock, who was heavily involved in recruiting informers, notes, most informers were satisfied with the simple gratification of having someone listening to them, the feeling that 'they were somebody' (p.201).

The combined efforts of official employees and unofficial informers generated an enormous web of intelligence and surveillance in the GDR. There was one officer or informer for every sixty-three people (p.57). With that kind of resourcing, the Stasi were able to accumulate and document amazing volumes of information. Funder notes that 'Laid out upright and end to end, the files the Stasi kept on their countrymen and women would form a line 180 kilometres long' (p.5). In the days leading up to the fall of the Wall, the Stasi made a frenzied attempt to destroy the masses of documents they had accrued. In 1990, the Stasi File Authority made the remaining files available to the GDR's former citizens. Several of the characters in *Stasiland* take up the opportunity to explore what Funder describes as their 'stolen biographies' (p.272): Klaus keeps copies in his bookshelf; Miriam consults the documents on herself and her husband in search of answers about Charlie's mysterious death in custody; even Mielke, just days before his death, requests access to his file. This last example demonstrates the reach of the Stasi and the effectiveness of its operations. The system Mielke had created was 'so thorough ... that somewhere, someone was keeping tabs' on the very man who was primarily responsible for it (p.254).

GENRE, STRUCTURE & LANGUAGE

Genre

Stasiland is an example of literary journalism, a hybrid kind of writing that blends the techniques of literary fiction with factual content. *Stasiland* is essentially a history, but it follows the conventions of fiction more closely than it does those of traditional historiography (the scholarly writing of history based on the critical assessment of various sources). Funder's deviation from traditional modes of writing about the past is important to the success of the project she attempts in *Stasiland*, and for effectively communicating some of the text's central ideas.

Funder articulates the motivation behind *Stasiland* at two key points in the text. At the chaotic swimming pool, Anna states that her research and writing is an attempt to make 'portraits of people, East Germans, of whom there will be none left in a generation' (p.147). Then, in her letter to Miriam, she explains that while she set out to tell Miriam's story she quickly realised that 'other things' needed to be explained, and other stories explored and told (p.246). Like the puzzlers, Funder is reconstructing the lives of citizens of the former GDR. To achieve this, she needs narrative space to construct full and believable characters and to let those characters speak in their own voices.

Sharing stories in this way creates particular narrative demands. For the stories to be comprehensible and believable, and for their full impact to be communicable, the characters must be portrayed in both the present and the past. Funder introduces a complex narrative timeframe, again making use of a fiction-writing technique. *Stasiland*'s narrative present is predominantly 1996, when Anna visits Berlin to research Miriam's story. (The concluding chapters are set in 2000.) Many of the events recounted by Anna or by the people she interviews occurred in the past, in the 1960s, 1970s or 1980s. Funder manages this delicate oscillation through a carefully crafted narrator.

Anna, a character that represents Funder in the text, is *Stasiland*'s narrator. Anna speaks in a first-person active voice to detail events that occur in the text's narrative present. Her conversations with Miriam, her travels on Berlin's trains and her drinking bouts with Klaus, for example, are all conveyed in an active voice; that is, she favours sentences in which the subject performs the action of the sentence, as in 'I want to ask but I sit tight' (p.33). However, Funder uses a third-person omniscient voice to detail facts and figures about the GDR in, for example, the paragraphs devoted to describing the parcelling up of territory by the Allies at the end of World War II (p.160) or the final days of the GDR in November 1989 (pp.67–71). At other times, Anna seems to disappear altogether as the author allows characters such as Julia, Miriam and Frau Paul to tell their own stories. This technique allows Funder to separate the narrative present from the past that informs it, while also conveying the idea that the past is never really over.

Funder's insertion of a first-person narrator represents another break from conventional historiography. Funder places herself – her own subjectivity, vulnerability and fallibility – in her text by introducing Anna as her representative on the page. Anna is keenly aware of her limited capacity to understand the GDR. She often makes direct judgements about people and situations, declaring that Frau Paul 'overestimated her own strength' (p.221), for example, or that the absence of the Wall is problematic. This kind of overt judgement is typically absent in historiography or in conventional journalism, both genres concerned chiefly with objectivity and facts. While facts are important to Funder, the meanings and consequences of those facts matter more. Crafting *Stasiland* as literary journalism gives Funder the space and opportunity to explore and elucidate consequences.

Structure

The structure of *Stasiland* supports the contention that 'history is made of personal stories' (p.13). The text is structured around Funder's attempts to understand one person's story – Miriam's. Anna's two meetings with Miriam bookend the text: the opening chapter documents Anna's first introduction to Miriam's history and her trip to Leipzig to meet her, while the concluding chapter details Anna's second meeting with Miriam three years later. In between these two chapters, Funder introduces a number of other characters with equally harrowing and extraordinary tales as Anna discovers that, to comprehend and communicate Miriam's story, she needs to 'explain other things around it' (p.246).

Each of *Stasiland*'s chapters is devoted to telling one person's story. Some stories, such as those belonging to Julia, Frau Paul and Hagen Koch, are depicted over several chapters. However, each story is self-contained. None cross over with another. This structuring technique has two significant effects. Firstly, it conveys the sheer extent of the damage inflicted by the Stasi. There are simply so many important and distinct stories to tell, despite Uwe's wondering how Anna managed to find all these people (p.120). Secondly, it confers enormous respect upon the storytellers. Each is given their own space. This humanising strategy contrasts sharply with the degrading and demeaning tactics employed by the Stasi that are so vividly illustrated in the text.

Funder's focus on elucidating personal histories results in a text that is structured more around themes and ideas, and less around the facts and chronologies that are important in formal history. For example, while the building of the Wall obviously occurred decades before its demolition, Funder describes the November 1989 fall of the Wall early in *Stasiland*, many chapters before she recounts its construction. Far from being confusing, this structuring technique enhances the reader's understanding of events and situations because these are explained in context. The description of the fall of the Wall is provided when Anna visits Stasi HQ, the site of the 1989 demonstrations. The description of its construction is given when Anna meets Hagen Koch who, in 1961, 'painted the line where the Wall would go' (p.155).

The structure also helps support some of the text's key themes and ideas. The meandering structure might defy the chronological conventions of formal historiography, but it replicates two human processes that are very important to Funder: conversation and memory. Conversation and memory, like the structure Funder employs in *Stasiland*, are episodic and organic. They are composed of connected ideas and events and do not adhere to a strict linear timeline. Listening to Julia recount her tragic history, Anna observes that 'memories do not come in the right order' (p.97). Arguably, the chapters of *Stasiland* are not in the 'right order' if the reader is desirous of a careful chronicle of events. But as Funder is concerned with personal stories, with the significance of facts rather than with the bare facts themselves, the winding, anachronous composition is an effective and compelling structuring technique.

Language

Literary journalism, the genre that best describes *Stasiland*, is a kind of creative nonfiction in which the creativity exists in the style of the writing itself, rather than in imagined plots and characters. Funder's vivid language establishes *Stasiland* as an instance of literary journalism and brings her characters and settings to life. Her language is highly descriptive, frequently figurative and extraordinarily precise.

Funder describes a vanished world, a world that, even when it existed, was so secret and bizarre that those who didn't live within it could barely have imagined it, let alone have comprehended it. Conveying this world is a challenge Funder responds to by using vivid, graphic language. The reader can easily imagine, for example, the horror of Hohenschönhausen on reading Funder's description of the smell of 'damp and old urine and vomit and earth: the smell of misery' (p.226), or the fanatical celebration of communist heroes with Funder's description of the 'god-like' busts 'with flowing hair' and the 'long row of clenched plaster fists sticking up for international socialism' (p.71) on display at Stasi HQ.

Funder's descriptions often incorporate metaphor and simile. Again, this can help render the foreign comprehensible, as evident in the descriptions of Hohenschönhausen's torture cells that liken contraptions to 'an apparatus at a county fair' (p.226) or 'some Pythonesque sideshow of history' (p.227). More frequently – and more powerfully – the alien landscape these figurative devices help Funder communicate is an emotional rather than a physical one. Julia is drawn as 'a hermit crab, all soft-fleshed with friends but ready to whisk back into its shell at the slightest sign of contact' (p.90). Frau Paul is a 'lonely, teary guilt-wracked wreck' (p.221). Simile and metaphor help Funder to draw vibrant, identifiable and believable characters and simultaneously to communicate the enormity of the pain and loss that those characters have experienced.

Funder's language is also extremely precise. She records the smallest detail about people and their environments, even of incidental background characters such as the beautiful cross-eyed mother with the pierced nose aboard the train to Potsdam (p.149) and the cigarette-smuggling Vietnamese flower vendor whom Anna encounters before visiting Frau Paul (p.204). In sharing Julia's story, Funder gives minute detail about the sparse apartment, the food consumed by the friends and the fading light in the room. The same attention to detail is used when recording Anna's conversations with Frau Paul, Miriam and Klaus, as well as with insiders such as von Schnitzler, with his 'thermos of hot water', 'jar of Nescafé' and 'large wineglass of something that looks like red cordial' (p.129). This level of detail is important to Funder's project. Precision helps rebuild the lives of these people who were so damaged by the regime. Funder's language gives their lives a richness and respect that they were denied under the Stasi. In this way, her language choices replicate the assiduousness of the unofficial biographies Stasi officers composed in their kilometres of files, but reinstate the respect and individuality that those documents denied and destroyed.

CHAPTER-BY-CHAPTER ANALYSIS

Berlin, Winter 1996 (pp.1–9)

Summary: *Anna travels to Leipzig to meet Miriam.*

The text starts in a train station, a transitory setting that immediately establishes Anna as a visitor and observer. Anna's hangover makes her see her surroundings oddly. Colours are too bright, smells too sharp, and the station is populated with slightly menacing people. This setting prepares the reader for the bizarre and disconcerting realities that Funder will explore in the text. Anna's conversation with the woman in the station establishes Funder's narrative style – a knitting together of the narrator's immediate experience and third-person chronicling of East Germany's history. Anna's reverie on the train taking her to Leipzig performs a similar function. It introduces the text's key themes and characters, as well as necessary historical information about the Berlin Wall and the Stasi. Finally, Anna introduces a mystery, and so the reader is cleverly compelled to follow her into Stasiland.

Q How does this chapter prepare the reader for what will follow in *Stasiland*?

Q How are language and setting used to introduce key ideas and themes?

Key point

Funder always capitalises references to the Berlin Wall, even in the colloquial reference 'the Wall'. This is partly because the Berlin Wall is a proper noun, but also because capitalisation helps convey the significance of the Wall in the lives of Berliners.

Miriam (pp.10–18)

Summary: *Anna meets Miriam.*

Working at a West Berlin television service, Anna becomes frustrated at the establishment's reluctance – even refusal – to recognise the stories of former East Germans. Anna's will is strengthened by her correspondence with a viewer in Argentina, who angrily writes that 'history is made of personal stories' (p.13). With that principle in mind, Anna travels to Leipzig to meet Miriam. Miriam tells Anna of the protest pamphlets she and a friend wrote and distributed in 1968, a childish act that was considered sedition by the Stasi and brought Miriam under their investigation at just sixteen years of age.

Key vocabulary

Prague Spring: a temporary relaxation in socialist strictures in Czechoslovakia, another Eastern Bloc country, between January and August 1968.

Q What does the Stasi's investigation of Miriam reveal about the Stasi organisation?

Q What is the 'new tune' that Funder refers to in her metaphor about the Mercedes emblem?

Bornholmer Bridge (pp.19–30)

Summary: *Miriam attempts to scale the Wall.*

Miriam's investigations at Bornholmer Bridge provide a comprehensive picture of the Wall. At this spot, the Wall consisted of 'a wire mesh fence, a patrol strip, a barbed-wire fence, a twenty-metre-wide asphalt street for the personnel carriers and a footpath' (p.21) covering some 150 meters. Miriam's cool observation of these menacing features and her clearing of so many obstacles highlight her courage, intelligence and level-headedness. Nevertheless, she is caught and again imprisoned and interrogated by the Stasi, subjected this time to torturous sleep deprivation.

Q There are two distinct timeframes in this chapter – the present in which Anna interviews Miriam and the past that Miriam recounts. What techniques does Funder use to manage and unite these two timeframes?

Charlie (pp.31–46)

Summary: *Miriam and Charlie's life together is detailed; Charlie's death and funeral are recounted.*

Miriam documents the Stasi's tools and strategies for controlling East Germans. In prison, she was known only as a number and was required to ask permission for every small act. The home she shared with Charlie was routinely searched. Her name was blacklisted so that she was 'prohibited' (p.35) from work or study. Despite this, Miriam's recollections of life with Charlie are imbued with happiness, showing that some things could not be tarnished by the Stasi. The Stasi's enormous power, though, is clearly evident in the events following Charlie's death. The district attorney responsible for investigating Charlie's death lied without compunction; the funeral parlours followed Stasi directions to hide evidence; Charlie's body was tampered with. Miriam is still searching for answers, now battling a new government in united Germany that resists her appeals because it wants 'to stop thinking about the past' (p.45).

Q Anna is increasingly horrified in listening to Miriam's story. How does Funder convey this mounting horror? What effect does this create for the reader?

Q Miriam is a well-developed character. Charlie, however, is developed only sketchily. Why might this be?

The Linoleum Palace (pp.47–53)

Summary: *Julia is introduced; Anna places an advertisement in the newspaper.*

Anna's description of her Berlin apartment demonstrates that her inhabitation of this place – of the flat and of Berlin – is merely temporary.

Everything in the flat is 'utilitarian' (p.49). Anna makes no attempt to repair the broken blind or replace the lumpy couch. She declares to Julia she needs just 'a bed, a desk, a chair and a coffee pot' (p.48), bare fundamentals for surviving and writing. This reflects Anna's relationship to Berlin and to Germany more broadly. She is a visitor who cannot be at home in the country because she won't ever quite understand it. She is, however, curious 'about what it must have been like to be on the inside ... and then to have that world and your place in it disappear' (p.53). To satisfy her curiosity, Anna places an advertisement in the local paper seeking Stasi men for interview. This marks the beginning of her research and the shift from casual interest to dedicated investigation, an act of remembering that challenges the literal overwriting of history Anna observes in the streets of Mitte.

Q How is Julia characterised in this chapter? How does this prepare the reader for the more detailed exploration of her character that will come in later chapters?

Q Funder paints the setting in a palette of dull greys and drab browns. What is the effect of this?

Stasi HQ (pp.54–66)

Summary: *Anna visits the Stasi Headquarters in Lichtenberg; the end of the regime is explained.*

Anna's visit to the former Stasi Headquarters provides the backdrop for a detailed outline of Stasi history. Funder gives context to the setting – and to the text as whole – by presenting a timeline of key events, facts and figures concerning the Stasi's operations, and by outlining biographical information about the regime's leaders. These chunks of historical information occur thematically, rather than chronologically. We learn about the final days of the GDR in this chapter – before we have learned how the regime started – because its demise happened here at Stasi HQ. The tour guide is a device through which Funder delivers factual information about Mielke, the Stasi and the regime's downfall, a device which enables Funder to include background detail without veering from the narrative timeframe she employs to structure the text.

Q Anna poses a rhetorical question: 'How can I reward informers a second time around?' (p.55). Is she an objective investigator? Is that a strength or a shortcoming of the text?

The Smell of Old Men (pp.67–75)

Summary: *Anna continues to explore Stasi HQ; the end of the GDR is explained.*

The panicked destruction of the Stasi's 'most incriminating' files (p.67) is an example of the deliberate forgetting and falsification of history that troubles Anna. It also illustrates an ironic deficiency of the Stasi – they were so orderly that the sacks of documents can be reconstituted and read anyway, albeit through painstaking work. That work is undertaken by the Stasi File Authority, a body created to open the GDR's files 'on its people to its people' (p.71). This organisation is a rare example of purposeful and agreed remembering, and contrasts with the indecision about what to do with Hitler's bunker and the Palast der Republik on which Anna comments earlier (p.52).

Q Why does the tour group become uncomfortable and reluctant to finish the tour?

Q What techniques does Funder employ to develop the familiar yet bizarre setting of Mielke's private quarters?

Telephone Calls (pp.76–87)

Summary: *Klaus is introduced; Anna meets Herr Winz.*

Funder's characterisation of Herr Winz as an 'underconfident and unconvincing' man 'play-acting' at being a spy (p.85) and as a blustering old man with an absurdly unwavering belief in the second coming of socialism shows that Anna is not an objective narrator. She has existing ideas about Germany's recent history which she does not wish to change. Her incredulity at Herr Winz's definition of the *Insiderkomitee* exemplifies this attitude. This chapter shows that Anna's research is not about building a balanced and unbiased view of what occurred during the years of GDR – something Herr Winz assumes when he agrees to meet – but to understand how such a state came into being and was so easily maintained.

Q How does Funder use dialogue to develop character and mood in this chapter? What is the mood she creates?

Julia Has No Story (pp.88–97)

Summary: *Julia begins to tell her story.*

Prompted by Julia's box of love letters from an unlikely Italian boyfriend, Anna coaxes Julia to share her story of Stasi scrutiny. Funder uses two distinct techniques. In the first half of the chapter, Julia's story is communicated in a conversation between her and Anna. This dialogue highlights Anna's clumsy misunderstanding of Julia's comments and her growing fascination. In the second half, Funder employs a different narrative voice, one more akin to that employed in journalism or reportage (factual presentation with a journalistic style) than the first-person active voice used for the earlier dialogue. The effect of this is that Anna recedes into the background and the reader's attention is focused solely on Julia and her particular experience.

Key point

Julia's comment 'There are things I don't remember' (p.95) introduces a new dimension to Funder's contemplation of memory and forgetting. The phrase could indicate that events cannot be recalled – that no memory exists – or that *not* remembering is a deliberate practice. Already the text has given many examples of German history being deliberately 'not remembered', such as the renaming of streets, Major Maler's denial of knowledge of Charlie's case and the destruction of Stasi files.

Q What do the drunks and punks lingering in the park suggest about contemporary life in Berlin?

Q What is the significance of Anna's statement, 'I have come to think of this apartment as some kind of closed and self-sustaining universe ... I just keep to my tracks' (pp.89–90)?

The Italian Boyfriend (pp.98–105)

Summary: *Julia's relationship with her Italian boyfriend and the Stasi's apparent tampering with Julia's education are recounted.*

This chapter complicates Julia. In the previous chapter, she seemed vulnerable and lonely. Here, she is pragmatic and independent. She accepted the increased surveillance of her life as a matter of fact, she refused the Italian's initial advances because he imagined her an easy target, and then ended their relationship because she refused to be dependent on him. She also refuses to be a victim for Anna when the latter expresses outrage about the political exam university applicants were required to sit. The disparity between these two distinct interpretations of Julia builds suspense – how she could have changed so markedly? – and indicates the enormous damage Stasi coercion and surveillance could effect on its targets.

Q What does the scene in the Employment Office illustrate about life in the GDR?

Q In what ways did the Stasi seem to control Julia's life? What do these reveal about the organisation?

Major N. (pp.106–17)

Summary: *Julia has an interview with Major N.*

Julia recalls a traumatic meeting with Major N. who reveals, with a disturbing friendliness, the extent to which the Stasi had been observing

Julia. They have copies of every letter sent between her and her boyfriend. They know every subject she studied at school, her marks, and intimate details of her family life. Major N. shows Julia that the Stasi controls her, a status that makes Julia instantly feel 'separate from everybody' (p.112). Julia, however, has an unlikely victory. She refuses to become an informer and, through her threat to write to Honecker, breaks the Stasi's grip. But the victory comes too late. Julia is already broken, her faith in her country destroyed, her trust eroded, and her sense of autonomy and confidence obliterated.

Q How does Funder convey Major N.'s menace in this chapter?

The Lipsi (pp.118–28)

Summary: *Anna watches episodes of 'The Black Channel'.*

With Uwe's help, Anna views tapes of 'The Black Channel', in which vitriolic host Karl-Eduard von Schnitzler censured the west. Von Schnitzler's commentary often involved rhetorical acrobatics that could turn an act of inhumanity, such as the shooting of a young man who tried to scale the Wall, into an act of humanity. The ideas of altered reality, illusion and interpretation are raised in this chapter. Anna, accustomed to travelling Berlin by train, sees 'another world' (p.119) when she travels in Uwe's car. The bizarre conversation between the men in cardigans seems like an abstract theatre performance. Frau Anderson is disguised in make-up that 'departs, boldly and theatrically, from nature' (p.123). This catalogue of real fictions culminates in Anna's discovery of the Lipsi, the state-sanctioned dance which she describes as 'a bizarre hipless camel of a thing' (p.127).

Key vocabulary

Beckett: Irish writer Samuel Beckett, famous for his absurdist plays and fiction.

Key point

Anna tells Uwe she has been 'having Adventures in Stasiland ... a place where what was said was not real, and what was real was not allowed, where people disappeared behind doors and were never heard from again, or were smuggled into other realms' (p.120). Anna's 'Adventures in Stasiland' evoke *Alice's Adventures in Wonderland,* the well-known children's book by Lewis Carroll. In that book, Alice falls down a rabbit hole and is transported to a bizarre fantasy world where characters talk in riddles, logic is subverted and decisions lead to unforeseen and often frightening consequences. Carroll's 'Wonderland' is a literary model for the strange and sinister world Funder constructs in her exploration of the former East Germany.

Q How does this chapter develop the character of Uwe?

Q What is the impact of Funder's description of the television station building, and of East German architecture more generally?

Von Schni– (pp.129–38)

Summary: *Anna visits von Schnitzler.*

Carefully structured dialogue conveys the tension of Anna's interview with von Schnitzler. The dash in the chapter's title symbolises a disruption (and echoes Julia's joke about how quickly people turned off their televisions to avoid watching 'The Black Channel'). This grammatical technique is used frequently throughout the chapter to represent von Schnitzler's repeated interruptions. This, along with the short, sharp way in which von Schnitzler speaks, his outbursts and his emphatic exclamations, helps establish him as a bully. But Anna is not a victim. She also interrupts him, is insistent on getting her questions answered, and confidently negotiates von Schnitzler's impasses.

Q How are the ideas about disparate views of reality, highlighted in the previous chapter, developed in this chapter?

Q Is von Schnitzler more committed to the GDR or to communism? What does this reveal about power and truth in the GDR?

The Worse You Feel (pp.139–47)

Summary: *Julia shares the story of her rape.*

Again, the narrator disappears into the background to give Julia a voice in telling this most intimate and painful of stories. The sparse setting similarly sharpens the focus on Julia and her narrative. Julia's account accentuates her vulnerability, but also her resilience. After the rape and investigation she attends her friends' wedding, so as to not ruin their day. She tells her story without crying. She is a mentor to Anna, able to comment sagely on the two worlds she has known and to validate Anna's project. Anna's project becomes clear in this chapter, both to the reader and to herself. In the regulated chaos of the local swimming pool – a metaphor for the Germany Anna can never quite comprehend – Anna realises she is 'making portraits' and protecting a history that is in danger of being wilfully forgotten.

Key vocabulary

Tiresias: a figure from Greek mythology, a blind man regarded as the greatest of all mythological prophets.

Q What is the significance of Anna's observation, 'Her eyes ... have a dark shape in them. When it moves, I see that it is me' (p.144)?

Herr Christian (pp.148–54)

Summary: *Herr Christian takes Anna on a tour of Stasi sites.*

Generous Herr Christian drives Anna to the Stasi's 'Coding Villa', an old bunker and a border inspection point. This meeting could not be more different from Anna's covert rendezvous with Herr Winz, a contrast which helps Funder demonstrate that the Stasi attracted all kinds of people for all kinds of reasons. Herr Christian joined because 'it might lead to a bit of adventure' (p.150) and, despite his harsh treatment after the organisation's discovery of his affair, he enjoyed his work. Funder's likening of Herr Christian's smile to that of 'a gangster, or an angel' (p.149) illustrates the character's complexity. He appears easygoing, but unflinchingly sent would-be escapees back to Potsdam for certain imprisonment. He claims to have an unwavering respect for the law but he casually disregards a 'keep out' sign.

Q Looking at portraits in a photographer's studio window, Anna comments that she enjoys seeing the locals 'as they want to be seen' (p.148). How does this statement connect with the key themes and narrative strategies of the text?

Socialist Man (pp.155–67)

Summary: *Anna visits Hagen Koch's 'Wall Archive'; an explanation of the post–World War II division of Germany is given.*

This chapter examines questions about the nature of history. It suggests that, when considering history, it is difficult to extricate a beginning from an end. All stories are intertwined. Anna only wants to hear Koch's story, but because Koch holds that his story 'comes directly out of' his father's story (p.158), she is required to be patient. Anna is also dubious about Koch's deep box of plastic-wrapped memorabilia; she is reluctant to spend all afternoon following the narrative that connects each piece and doubts the capacity of the collected documents, which are simply facts, to tell a complete story. Nevertheless, Koch's kind of history is important. It represents evidence that testifies against the 'sleight-of-history' (p.161) and the quick remaking of history that Funder is so critical of in Germany's writing over of Nazism.

Q How does Funder use both reportage and fiction-style narrative to describe the Berlin blockade? What does this blend of narrative styles achieve?

Q Why is the story of his father important to understanding Koch? How does it illuminate more generally life in the GDR?

Drawing the Line (pp.168–76)

Summary: *The building of the Wall is described; the Stasi interferes in Koch's marriage.*

Funder describes the building of the Berlin Wall on 12 August 1961 through Koch, who painted the line marking where the structure would go. Koch voices the contemporaneously popular view about the Wall and shows that many ordinary people believed the Wall was necessary to protect the interests of the GDR. However, Koch is not an objective or entirely reliable narrator. The previous chapter demonstrated his complete inculcation in GDR ideology. Despite Koch's unwavering faith in the regime, though, he is cruelly punished for a misdemeanour. His predisposition to trust the Stasi over his wife shows the depth of his faith.

Key point

Koch's swift promotion to Director of the Drafting Office of Cartographics and Topography at Mielke's direct request presents an opportunity for Funder to ridicule the Stasi. Koch is a technical draftsman. He knows nothing about drawing geographical maps. This is the second time Funder has used a character to illustrate the shortcomings of the Stasi: Miriam's near escape, with no training and no assistance, has a similar effect. In both cases, Funder exposes the Stasi's pride and unwavering self-belief, the blind certainty that causes Stasi personnel to make comically misinformed decisions.

Q To 'draw the line' means to refuse to do something that you do not feel comfortable doing. How is this idiom illustrated in this chapter?

The Plate (pp.177–83)

Summary: *Koch steals a plastic plate.*

Koch's theft of the painted plastic plate from his Stasi office is an act of defiance and self-affirmation in the face of a system that wilfully dehumanises even its most faithful adherents. Funder carefully constructs the plate as a piece of junk by highlighting its cheapness and tackiness. Very real battles – a Stasi investigation, an argument with a television crew, and a criminal investigation and charges for perjury – are played out over this plate. Through sharing this anecdote, Funder shows that when people are robbed of autonomy, small things become major victories.

Q Funder visits Bornholmer Bridge with diagrams and photographs from Koch's collection and with Miriam's hand-drawn map. What does this demonstrate about the importance of documentary evidence in understanding history?

Klaus (pp.184–94)

Summary: *Klaus recounts his experiences with the Stasi.*

Klaus is relaxed in Anna's company. He greets her in a dressing gown, they drink beer together and, after only a moment's reluctance, he generously shares his story. This ease between the two helps emphasise Klaus' equanimity, a quality that sets him apart from other characters in the text, as does his capacity to forgive former Stasi personnel. He has reason to be angry. The Stasi forced his band out of existence, taking his identity, career and financial security with it. The Stasi's ability to obliterate the popular band overnight demonstrates their enormous power, and the extent to which their influence infiltrated every aspect of life in the GDR.

Key vocabulary

Ersatz: substitution, usually of inferior quality.

Q How does Funder convey Klaus' relaxed nature?

Q Klaus says the GDR was 'built on lies—lie after lie after lie' (p.187). What 'lies' are detailed in this chapter?

Herr Bock of Golm (pp.195–203)

Summary: *Anna meets Herr Bock; the Stasi's structure is detailed.*

This chapter explores motivations. From Herr Bock, Anna learns about 'the science of recruiting informers' (p.195), the barely paid and unaffiliated individuals who passed on information about 'kindergartens and dinner parties and sporting events' (p.200) to the Stasi. Anna wonders, without the security of a job or remuneration, 'What was in it for the informers?' (p.200). She concludes that the motivation is just 'the small deep human satisfaction of having one up on someone else' (p.201). The Stasi was so effective at breeding suspicion and isolation that betrayal became comfortable. Bock's overview of the Stasi's methods, of the increasingly broad definition of 'enemy' and of the infiltration of colleges and churches, shows how the Ministry established the conditions that produced the informers it wanted.

Q What is the mood of this chapter? What techniques does Funder use to create that mood?

Q How does this chapter expand the reader's understanding of the Stasi and its operations?

Frau Paul (pp.204–12)

Summary: *Frau Paul talks about being separated from her son.*

Frau Paul's sad tale illustrates the enormous suffering the Wall imposed on ordinary people, and the effects of that suffering. Funder thoroughly details baby Torsten's condition and his mother's escalating misery as the new border first denied him medicine and then his mother's company. In so doing, she shows the Wall's human impact. Frau Paul's resultant misery and frustration led her to attempt escape and her plans quickly involved her in a complicated smuggling operation, both actions she would never have considered before her forced separation from her infant son.

Q Why does Frau Paul's conversation 'become muddled' and 'peppered with statements' about what she didn't know (p.212)? What effect does this passage create?

Q Is Frau Paul a clearly drawn character at the end of this chapter? Why or why not?

The Deal (pp.213–21)

Summary: *Anna visits the tunnel used in Coch's escape attempt; Frau Paul recounts her arrest and the deal the Stasi offered her.*

This chapter complicates Frau Paul. The Stasi's surveillance of her activities and her summary arrest suggest her involvement in Coch's escape attempts was greater than she reveals to Anna. Her representation of herself as an unknowing casualty conflicts with Karl Wilhelm Fricke's knowledge and open admiration of her. Funder's earlier portrayal of her as a fragile housewife contrasts with the strength of character required to refuse the Stasi's deal. Funder's retreat from the conventions of historiography is particularly obvious in this chapter, as she attempts to reconcile these diverse aspects of Frau Paul's character. Far from being an objective observer, Funder offers interpretations of Frau Paul's actions and consequent emotional state.

Q Why is Anna so astonished by the sign advertising digging equipment?

Q What might the renovations of the apartment block symbolise? What does this passage suggest about memory and forgetting? What is the narrator's tone here?

Hohenschönhausen (pp.222–34)

Summary: *Frau Paul recounts her incarceration in Hohenschönhausen; Anna meets Torsten.*

Funder's matter-of-fact description of Hohenschönhausen – of its linoleum hallways, peeling paint and awful torture chambers – amplifies the prison's horror. She uses short, sharp sentences that help to make the setting seem terribly real, because the clear, unadorned language suggests that Anna simply states what she sees. Her verbatim inclusion of letters penned and posted by Torsten's nurses similarly conveys real misery, simply and without artifice. Funder does not exaggerate or embellish Frau Paul's experiences, an important technique in effectively communicating their dreadfulness. Some relief from the tragedy is offered by the introduction of Torsten, a relaxed adult who has a happy relationship with his mother and harbours no resentment for the choices she made.

Q Torsten is happy that the Wall is now invisible. Does his attitude pose a challenge for Funder? What does Anna learn from this conversation with Torsten?

Herr Bohnsack (pp.235–44)

Summary: *Anna meets Herr Bohnsack; Anna returns to Australia.*

Anna's meeting with Herr Bohnsack is very different from her meetings with the other Stasi men. Bohnsack is warm and relaxed and is prepared to talk openly in a public place. The setting for this meeting, and Funder's careful construction of the atmosphere, establishes Bohnsack as a man without 'anything to prove' (p.236). Through Bohnsack, Funder exposes a different aspect of the Stasi – the international espionage work conducted under the leadership of 'elegant intellectual' Markus Wolf (p.237). Herr Bohnsack's open ridicule of Mielke – both in the past and in his conversation with Anna – illustrates his courage and his willingness to think and act independently, a quality conspicuously absent in the other Stasi men.

Key vocabulary

Karla: the Russian spymaster in John le Carré's famous spy novel *Tinker, Tailor, Soldier, Spy* (1974).

Foutu: French slang meaning to be damned or completely destroyed.

Q What techniques does Funder use to convey Herr Bohnsack's openness?

Q In what other ways does this meeting differ from Anna's previous meetings with Stasi men? What does this suggest about Herr Bohnsack?

Berlin, Spring 2000 (pp.245–52)

Summary: *Anna returns to Berlin after a three-year absence; Anna talks with the drunks in the park.*

This is a chapter of new beginnings. Anna returns with renewed purpose. She resumes contact with Miriam and Julia. She notices small, homely changes in her apartment. Funder's vivid descriptions of Berlin in spring, which demonstrate an interest in the city's natural landscape entirely absent earlier, intensify this sense of promise. This feeling of fresh possibility, however, is countered by Professor Mushroom's wistful *ostalgie* (nostalgia for the GDR). He laments the loss of the comforts and protections of the GDR – its cheap beer, universal healthcare and affordable rent. These arguments, which Anna has heard before, show that not everyone happily embraces unified Germany's capitalism.

Q What is the tone of the scene in the park? How does Funder create this tone? What is its effect?

Q Professor Mushroom believes that 'if you didn't buck the system, then it wouldn't harm you' (p.252). Based on what Funder has documented so far, do you agree or disagree with that argument? Why?

The Wall (pp.253–61)

Summary: *Anna tours the Wall with Koch.*

Anna's tour of the Wall – or what is left of it – with Koch raises questions about the politics of memory. How should history be remembered?

Whose version should be remembered? Anna is dissatisfied with the new museum and its 'sanitised Disney version' (p.256) of the Wall. Koch is incensed that the plaques inlaid in the footpath, marking where the Wall stood, are written for the western point of view. That history is high stakes is also illustrated by the threatening opposition to Frau Paul's campaigns for compensation and to preserve Hohenschönhausen, by von Schnitzler's fury and fear about the desecration of Mielke's grave, and by Gerd's profiteering through selling dubious relics to western tourists.

Q In what ways does this chapter prepare for the text's conclusion?

Q What is the significance of Koch's story about the Turkish onions?

Q Is the Wall less real now that it is almost completely gone?

Puzzlers (pp.262–9)

Summary: *Anna visits the Stasi File Authority.*

Anna's high hopes for the puzzlers are disappointed by the reality of the operation. The realisation about just how slow the process is – reflected in Anna's observation of the 'masses and masses of tiny pieces of paper' laid in stacks on desks and filing cabinets – makes her 'panicked' (p.264). Anna's fears about the magnitude of the puzzlers' task are confirmed by Herr Raillard's note. The bitterness of her disappointment is captured in the simile likening the operation to 'something between a hobby farm for jigsaw enthusiasts and a sheltered workshop for obsessives' (p.265).

Q All the puzzlers are westerners. What does their tearoom conversation about the former GDR reveal about western attitudes to life in the east?

Miriam and Charlie (pp.270–82)

Summary: *Anna returns to Leipzig to visit Miriam.*

Against a backdrop of renovation and reconstruction, Anna visits Miriam in Leipzig. Miriam is still searching for answers, but is now able to talk about Charlie and what might have happened the night he died. This represents a new beginning for Miriam, one subtly indicated by the chapter's title, which figuratively reunites Miriam and Charlie. By returning to Miriam and by visiting the shabby museum at Runde Ecke, Anna has come full circle. She has 'nothing more to do' (p.272) but to observe the young people strolling Leipzig's streets and playing in the park near her apartment. In this closing scene, Anna notices swings and roundabouts and children for the first time, images of hope and promise.

Key point

Funder's project – to give voice to ordinary people – is confirmed in this chapter. Exhibitions within the Contemporary History Forum feature many of the same characters and settings that populate the text: Klaus, von Schnitzler, Frau Paul's tunnel and paddy wagon. But the exhibitions, pinned behind glass, are safe and sanitised, lacking the depth and humanity that Funder is able to confer by telling individuals' stories in vivid, compelling prose.

Q What are the differences between the two museums? Why does Anna prefer the older, smaller museum?

Q 'New facades of buildings in sun-yellow and dusky pink, some even gilded, have been revealed from behind scaffolding' (p.270). What is the significance of the renovations?

CHARACTERS & RELATIONSHIPS

Anna

Key quotes

'I like the freedom of being suspended between two places' (p.281)

'*What am I doing here?*' (p.147)

It is useful to understand Anna as a character distinct from Funder because this helps differentiate the author's ideas and techniques from the character's adventures and activities. Anna, an Australian writer, visits Germany in 1996 after an earlier visit to West Berlin left her wondering 'long and hard what went on behind that Wall' (p.4). She is curious and empathetic, qualities that render her a complex narrator. She is a skilled interviewer, a trusted confidante, and an intelligent, scathing critic of the Stasi.

For all her skills and qualities, Anna is an observer inevitably removed from the subjects she researches. Julia casually points out Anna's foreignness when she states that Anna's pale skin and eyes 'don't look German' (p.91). As a visitor, Anna is occasionally confused by the implicit meaning of stories she hears. For example, Miriam needs to explain to Anna her implausible account of her escape attempt (p.28). Anna's tenuous occupation of the sparsely furnished rented apartment and her occasional hypersensitivity (demonstrated by her instant outrage at hearing of Julia's failing the University's political exam, for example) also emphasise her remoteness from the society she investigates.

Anna's distance informs her judgement. She is occasionally too quick to ascribe the failings she perceives in the state and the society to 'Germanness'. But her remove is also advantageous. Anna's distance from the Stasi makes her inquisitive and inspires her desire to hear and share the stories of ordinary people that her colleagues cursorily dismiss.

Key point

Anna unifies disparate stories. With the exception of Julia and Klaus, all major characters are people Anna meets through her research and they appear in the text only as she interviews them. No relationships exist between *Stasiland*'s major characters; Anna's narration brings them together.

Miriam Weber

Key quotes

'In her voice is a combination of pride in how she became such a fiend, and disbelief that this country created enemies of its own children.' (p.15)

'I couldn't say to someone, "I'll meet you on Sunday"—I found that sort of thing an unbearable obligation.' (p.277)

'For Miriam, the past stopped when Charlie died.' (p.44)

Miriam's story inspires *Stasiland*. As Anna notes in a letter to Miriam, 'I tried to write your story, but found I needed to explain other things around it' (p.246). Those 'other things' are explained in the chapters between Anna's two meetings with Miriam, and so Miriam's sad, strange story underpins everything that is explored and elucidated in the text.

Miriam became an 'Enemy of the State' at sixteen (p.15) after she and a friend published and distributed pamphlets criticising the Leipzig police's treatment of protesters. In the East Germany of 1968, this was no simple act of teenage high-mindedness. It was 'the crime of sedition' (p.17). At that point, Miriam had no serious opposition to the state, but the chain of events that followed – her arrest and interrogation, escape attempt, second arrest, and imprisonment in a brutal women's prison – confirmed her contempt for the Stasi. Miriam's experiences illustrate two damnable aspects of the Stasi: its stubborn, dangerous pride and its ability to inflict severe and lasting harm on its own citizens.

Miriam's near escape humiliated the Stasi. It was 'beyond comprehension that a sixteen-year-old with no tools, no training, and no help' could scale the Wall (p.25). Embarrassed Stasi personnel responded harshly, subjecting the child to ten days' interrogation and to torturous sleep deprivation in their determination to obtain an explanation. They would not – could not – believe the truth. Ironically, so blinded by their desperation to be right, they accepted her ridiculous fiction.

The suffering she endured during this interrogation – and would later endure in prison, in the incessant surveillance of her life, and in coping with Charlie's death – left Miriam with many 'little tics' (p.32). She cannot plan ahead or make commitments, as Anna discovers in her numerous attempts to pin Miriam down. Her door-less, top-storey apartments with sweeping views demonstrate her unusual need for space. She chain smokes. She 'has no partner in life' because it is too hard to explain her past and her habits (p.280). This catalogue of 'tics' demonstrates the lasting damage the Stasi's actions could cause.

Miriam is 'brave and strong and broken all at once' (p.44). Her strength and courage are illustrated by her preparedness to stand up to cemetery officials, Stasi officers and district attorneys. The contrast between Anna's two meetings with Miriam – three years apart – also affirms her strength and resilience. When they first meet, Miriam is clothed all in black. She cuts herself out of her own wedding photographs and, though she is generous with her story, when she speaks 'it is as if her existence is no longer real to her' (p.44). In the final chapter, Miriam dresses in flowing white and lives in a new apartment where 'Everything is white and light and comfortable' (p.274). She talks of her own life and work and shows Anna photographs of herself with Charlie, having looked through Charlie's papers for the first time since he died. Miriam is still looking for answers, but has begun to make peace with her past.

Julia Behrend

Key quotes

'a woman ... only part-attached to the world' (p.97)

'she associates the fall of the Wall with the end of what had remained of her private sphere after the Stasi had finished with it' (p.144)

'They honour their victims here ... I'm sure it could go too far, but for me, now, it is a good thing.' (p.246)

Anna's landlord Julia randomly visits Anna's apartment to remove bookshelves and boxes of old love letters. It is through the letters that Anna discovers that Julia, despite her protestations to the contrary, has her own story of the Stasi.

Like Miriam, Julia was subjected to Stasi scrutiny as a teenager. The Stasi intercepted, copied and filed every letter sent between her and her Italian boyfriend. Stasi men listened in to the lovers' telephone calls and searched them whenever they ventured out in public together. The Stasi also interfered with Julia's education, sending the talented student to a far-flung boarding school of 'no reputation' (p.100) and denying her entry into university. The Ministry then tampered with her job prospects, leaving her unemployed in a country where unemployment was pronounced nonexistent. The Stasi created a fiction out of Julia's life, thereby denying her autonomy. Julia's loss of self-determination is compounded by two violent episodes: her chilling interview with Major N. and her rape.

Consequently, Julia reacts strongly to perceived aggressors, and imagines the park's impotent drunks as a threat. Like Miriam, she dresses in 'layers of black' (p.90), 'regards fixed appointments as intolerable constraints on her freedom' (p.49) and is 'unable to go forward into her future' (p.95). She resembles Miriam in her resilience as well as her damage. She refused to marry her boyfriend, even though the marriage guaranteed escape, because she loathed the idea of being 'utterly dependent on him' (p.105). She attended her friends' wedding the morning after her brutal rape. Later, she moves to San Francisco to start a new life where she can work through the idea of her victimhood rather than be defined by it.

The key difference between Julia and Miriam is their attitude to the state. Julia was born into a regime solidified and protected by the Wall. She was raised by loyalist parents, had utter faith in the GDR and even had aspirations to work for it (p.96). She lived with the Stasi's intense scrutiny 'as a fact' and ridiculed her boyfriend's terror (p.99). She 'had never wanted' to leave (p.114). Her experiences, though, led to disillusionment. She realised that the GDR was not 'the good father state' in which she believed, but something 'so very dangerous' that destroyed its own faithful without them having 'done anything at all' (p.114). Julia exemplifies lost trust and highlights a terrible flaw in the Stasi's operations: they were so blinded by their need to control individuals that they undermined loyalty and faith where it existed.

Key point

The many similarities between Anna and Julia – their age, looks, talent for language and teenage flings with Italian boyfriends – render Julia Anna's East German *doppelgänger* (double). Their similarity decreases Anna's distance from the events she relates and the effects of Stasi operations because she is able to imagine herself within that otherwise foreign context.

Frau Sigrid Paul (Rührdanz)

Key quotes

'I had to decide against my son, but I couldn't let myself be used' (p.220)

'the picture she has of herself is one that the Stasi made for her' (p.229)

'Spic and span' Frau Paul, with her tidy house and 'exquisite open sandwiches' (p.205), is arguably the most damaged of *Stasiland*'s characters. As she recounts her piteous story of being separated from her critically ill infant son and her injurious incarceration in Hohenschönhausen, Frau Paul reads from 'notes on her own life' (p.205) and frequently wipes away tears with a neatly pressed handkerchief. The great tragedy Anna perceives is that Frau Paul views herself as the Stasi constructed her – as a criminal.

The disparity between this self image and her public one also renders Frau Paul one of the text's most intriguing characters. Frau Paul is famous. When Anna tells the tour guide at Stasi HQ that she wants to interview 'people who confronted the regime', the guide responds 'you need to meet Frau Paul' (p.71). Michael Hinze describes Frau Paul as a 'very courageous woman' (p.228) and credits her instrumentality in smuggling young defectors to the west. She is also dubbed 'a *very* brave woman' (p.220) by her own hero, Karl Wilhelm Fricke, a famous journalist. Yet Frau Paul is silent about this identity, claiming to have been entirely unaware of the escape syndicate operating around her.

The aspects of her story that she does share, however, are enough to establish her as courageous by her own telling. After a twenty-two-hour interrogation in a Stasi prison, perched on a stool 'designed for indignity' (p.219), Frau Paul is offered a deal: inform on Michael Hinze and travel freely to the west to visit Torsten. Frau Paul refuses. To refuse is courageous enough, but to choose her conscience over her son is extraordinarily brave, a decision that 'took a whole new fund of courage to live with' (p.221).

The ramifications of that decision illustrate the consequences of courage. Frau Paul is eventually reunited with her son, but only after being broken by her four-year imprisonment and the destruction of her family life. Torsten returns so institutionalised that his manners are overly formal, signalling a 'terrible distance' (p.231) that continues to pain Frau Paul. Anna speculates that Frau Paul, still tearfully defending her decision, has merely traded one terrible guilt for another. For all her principles and fortitude, Frau Paul is now 'a lonely, teary guilt-wracked wreck' (p.221).

Klaus Renft

Key quotes

'the bad boy of East German rock 'n' roll' (p.185)

'He seems incapable of regret, and anger evaporates off him like sweat.' (p.191)

Klaus is an ageing rock star, 'the legendary "Mik Jegger" of the Eastern Bloc' (p.80) and Anna's drinking companion. He is the only non-Stasi male character in *Stasiland* and has a very different attitude toward the Stasi from Miriam, Julia and Frau Paul. He gets 'distinct pleasure from the story-telling' in his file (p.188) and keeps copies of his unofficial biography in folders on his lounge-room shelf. He has no interest in pursuing Stasi personnel, claiming that they have been sufficiently punished by their own consciences (p.192), and is nonchalant, even amused, by his encounters with the Ministry.

This attitude highlights Klaus' unusual 'gift of taking things easy' (p.191) rather than diminishes the harm done by the Stasi. Klaus did suffer at its hands. The Ministry obliterated Klaus' band – the wildly popular Klaus Renft Combo – overnight, removing its records from shops and radio playlists, banning press coverage and forcing the recording company that produced Renft's music to reprint its 'entire catalogue' to exclude the band (p.190). Klaus was left 'with nothing to do, no-one to do it with' (p.191), removed to the west where he was a nobody. Klaus eschews recriminations and claims to have been protected by 'some kind of naivety' (p.192). But Anna observes a determined self-preservation, a 'carefully nurtured and maintained' naivety and 'an innocence that he did not let them damage' (p.192). That the unusually easygoing Klaus is the only character to display such resilience highlights the damage the Stasi could inflict on ordinary people.

Karl-Eduard von Schnitzler

Key quotes

> 'a grumpy old puppet throwing scorn on proceedings from on high' (p.122)

The veteran television presenter haughtily describes himself as 'one of the leading figures of the GDR' (p.132), ascribing huge importance to his television show 'The Black Channel'. Von Schnitzler's self-importance is challenged, however, by Anna's anecdote about the power back-surge that occurred every night 'as everyone, simultaneously, switched off' (p.121).

Anna's interview with von Schnitzler proves the appraisal made by Frau Anderson at the East German television station that he has 'stuck with what he said back then' (p.123). Even at seventy-nine, and having lived in a capitalist state for almost a decade, von Schnitzler's faith in the regime is steadfast. His stubborn, zealous belief in the Wall as 'humane' (p.134) and 'necessary to defend a threatened nation' (p.137), and in Mielke as 'the most humane human being' (p.137), shows how ideological fervour created bizarre realities in the GDR.

Herr Winz

Key quotes

> 'this man wants to play spy games seven years after the fall of the Wall' (p.81)

Anna's first Stasi man disguises himself as a westerner for their covert meeting, in which he hopes 'to set the record straight' (p.80). Bereft of the identity he enjoyed in the GDR, Herr Winz clings to his Stasi role through his membership of the *Insiderkomitee* and comforts himself through conversations with people who claim that socialism offered more safety and security than the capitalism that took its place. He also clings, hopelessly, to 'the Second Coming of socialism' (p.86). Unlike the other Stasi men Anna meets, Herr Winz is cagey about his past and reluctant to share detail. Together with his blustering about a second revolution and devotion to the *Insiderkomitee,* this creates a character pathetically out of touch.

Herr Christian

Key quotes

'He looks straight at me, smiling his lopsided smile like a gangster, or an angel.' (p.149)

Non-ideological Herr Christian joined the Stasi to box for the organisation's sporting club, and recalls his time with 'the Firm' as an amusing adventure. With his jeans, black BMW and wiry blond curls, Herr Christian's meeting with Anna has the casualness of a date. But there is something unnerving about him, a disquiet succinctly conveyed by the simile about his smile. Herr Christian claims to have 'an acute sense of duty to obey the law' (p.150) and to be a stickler for rules. Nevertheless, he has an adulterous relationship which he keeps secret from the Stasi. He is demoted and harbours a grudge against the friend with 'an overdeveloped sense of loyalty' who informed on him (p.152). He also claims to be sensitive but dispassionately sent would-be escapees – including women and children – back to Potsdam for certain imprisonment.

Hagen Koch

Key quotes

'a lone crusader against forgetting' (p.259)

'a poster boy for the new regime' (p.165)

'the Wall is the thing that defined him, and he will not let it go' (p.257)

As a twenty-one-year-old recruit, exuberant Hagen Koch was the man who marked out where the Wall would be built (p.171). He runs, with an energetic dedication to documentary evidence, a 'Wall Archive' comprised of photographs, maps, newspaper articles and other mementos commemorating the Wall from the eastern side. The fervour with which he collects and catalogues artefacts illustrates a commitment to memory and a belief that events are interconnected over time. His longwinded explanation of how he joined the Stasi, which sees him delving into a deep cardboard box of plastic-wrapped articles, tests Anna's patience. It also tests her project. This period in Germany's history cannot be viewed in isolation from what came before.

Koch's personal history reveals a lot about the Stasi and their methods. Koch was thoroughly indoctrinated as the perfect socialist child due to his father's coercion by local officials. Through him, Funder is able to convey the fictions unquestioning citizens accepted as fact, like the suppositions that the Wall would stop western profiteering and that the Americans were deliberately damaging East German crops.

Like Julia, Koch lost his unwavering faith in the GDR because of the Stasi's treatment of him. Koch was arrested on the trumped-up charge of 'Preparation and Reproduction of Pornographic Material' (p.173) after he tried to leave the Stasi. The innocent nature of Koch's indictable activity – producing crude cartoons for a friend's wedding – is reminiscent of Miriam's naive protest pamphlets. The Stasi forced Koch's wife to sign divorce papers, documents he was incapable of doubting, and forced him to retract his resignation. Betrayed by the organisation he believed in, he shifted his devotion to memorialising the Wall.

Herr Bock

Key quotes

'He is enjoying himself, here in the dark.' (p.203)

Herr Bock taught 'the science of recruiting informers' (p.195) at the Ministry's training academy, and uses his knowledge and skills to educate Anna about the Stasi's formal structure. Like Herr Winz, he uses Stasi conventions in the interview, informing Anna that she must not use his name (p.196). His undeviating subscription to 'perfect dictator-logic' (p.199) also shows that he still firmly adheres to Stasi beliefs. As with Herr Winz, the way in which he is characterised by Funder undermines Herr Bock's Stasi-acquired power. The description of him 'sitting camouflaged in ... a beige-and-brown diamond pattern acrylic cardigan' (p.196) with 'His feet, in socks and sandals, barely touch[ing] the floor' (p.198) makes him appear childish, impotent and faintly pathetic. He is an old man whose time to do damage has passed.

Herr Bohnsack

Key quotes

'He is not, as it turns out, a man with anything to prove.' (p.236)

Herr Bohnsack is unlike the other Stasi men Anna interviews. His name is openly listed on his apartment door. He meets Anna in public, taking her to his local bar where the publican smiles at him 'like a brother' (p.236). There is no secrecy, no pretence. This contrast results from two things. Firstly, Herr Bohnsack was employed in a different division from Anna's other interviewees, belonging to Division X under the command of the 'intelligent and urbane' Markus Wolf (p.236). Secondly, he 'outed himself' (p.236), taking his story – complete with a photograph – to a local magazine in the days immediately after the Wall fell. This history gives Herr Bohnsack the ability to be relaxed and open with Anna and to joke about the Stasi, but it also leaves him isolated. When Anna asks who his friends are, he answers 'I have none' (p.243). Herr Bohnsack, for all his courage and independence, is also a lonely victim of the Stasi.

Key point

Through the five Stasi men, Funder exposes the range of reasons people had for joining the Stasi. Every man had a distinct motivation, but Anna also makes her own assumptions about an unconscious, common motivation: 'In a society riven into "us" and "them", an ambitious young person might well want to be one of the group in the know, one of the unmolested' (p.156).

THEMES, IDEAS & VALUES

Courage

Key quotes

'I was trying, I think, to get a perspective on this lost world, and the kinds of courage in it.' (p.246)

'It is so hard to know what kind of mortgage our acts put on our future.' (p.221)

Funder examines how ordinary people coped in the GDR's extraordinary circumstances and, because she portrays her major characters as survivors, the text illuminates many acts of courage. *Stasiland* identifies and explores two broad kinds of courage: resistance to the regime and the resilience to survive its effects.

Resistance

Stasiland vividly illustrates the power of the Stasi and shows various ways in which courageous individuals resisted the Firm. Miriam, as the text's central character, is important in developing this theme. Anna admires the youthfully indignant Miriam who voices her outrage at the Leipzig police's treatment of protestors in a leaflet demanding state 'consultation' with citizens (p.16). Miriam's later actions prove that this was no mere act of frivolous teenage rebellion. Her cool scrutiny of the Wall and its plethora of protective armaments at Bornholmer Bridge, and her determined progress in overcoming so many of those obstacles, show that Miriam was a conspicuously courageous teenager. That courage helped her resist her Stasi interrogators and enables her, as an adult, to thwart the Stasi's interference in Charlie's funeral and to continually demand answers from Major Maler and the district attorney tasked with investigating Charlie's death in newly unified Germany.

Stasi insiders also resist the Ministry's excesses. Herr Bohnsack broke the Stasi's 'code of honour' by outing himself in the local press, choosing to share his history on his own terms rather than adhere to the party line (p.242). Herr Christian refused to let the Stasi take his privacy. He kept his extramarital affair secret because, despite describing himself as a stickler for rules, he always believed that 'some things are private' (p.152). Hagen Koch refused to let the Stasi take his pride. Bitter about the manner of his leaving the Firm, at the ease with which he would be replaced and at knowing that his years of loyal service 'would leave no mark', Koch stole a plastic plate from his office in an act of 'private revenge' (p.178). Koch laments that the plate – a cheap, plastic piece of junk – 'was all I had the courage for' (p.178), a statement that underlines the ultimate futility of the acts of internal resistance documented in the text. While each act demanded enormous courage, Herr Bohnsack's, Herr Christian's and Koch's rebellions are small, individual and ineffective at bringing about change.

More triumphant outcomes arise from fortitude, and it is this sustained courage, rather than opportunistic bravery, that Funder portrays as effectual, if only to a limited extent. The Stasi had to drop the charges of 'Deception of the Ministry' (p.29) against Miriam because, beaten by Miriam's tenacity, they had gathered false evidence through illegal means. Julia's courage in writing to Honecker had a similar result. Major N.'s dubious method was exposed and, 'sweating and uncomfortable', he released Julia from her ensnarement (p.116). Frau Paul's courage, too, enabled her to enjoy a triumph over the Stasi. She refused to 'be used' (p.220) as an informer, choosing to walk into her future with a clear conscience whatever the personal cost demanded by that choice.

The ambiguity of Frau Paul's victory, however, encapsulates Funder's attitude to resistance. Almost all resistance was ineffectual in terms of its impact on the regime. Victories were small and private. No defiance exhibited by any of the characters brought down the state or had any lasting impact on the Stasi. Frau Paul's victory, like Julia's and Miriam's, was effectual only on a personal level. Funder values the personal consequences of fortitude, but recognises that no individual – however brave – could truly weaken the Stasi's power.

Resilience

Resilience – the capacity to withstand the damages inflicted by the Stasi – is a kind of courage valued by Funder and one that underpins her investigation of life in the former GDR: her admiration of characters who demonstrate resilience is central to the text. As an act of 'life-giving' (Shakespeare 2003), *Stasiland* celebrates survivors and affirms their capacity to move forward. Even the text's most damaged characters exhibit resilience. Julia, made lonely and unpredictable by her injurious encounters with the Stasi, has the fortitude to attend her friends' wedding just hours after being raped and then humiliated in a callous police investigation. Almost entirely bereft of autonomy after the Stasi denies her education and employment, she refuses to marry her 'controlling' (p.105) Italian boyfriend because she wants to be able to determine her own life. While Julia's inability to work or study full-time, to make friends and to maintain the regular hours of normal people, suggests she has little success in managing her own life, her move to America demonstrates a positive change. At first mistrustful and apparently 'unable to go forward into her future' (p.95), by the text's conclusion Julia has commenced a promising new life in San Francisco, where she has made friends, works in a feminist bookshop and marches in 'Reclaim the Night' processions. She has evidently retained the agency she so valued as a teenager, despite the incursions of the Stasi and other aggressors into her private sphere.

Funder's characterisation of Frau Paul illustrates similarly extraordinary resilience. Frau Paul is initially depicted as a weeping wreck of a woman who is tortured by her decision, even though Torsten holds no grudge toward his parents. However, her ability to work as a tour guide at the prison that broke her, her active campaigning to preserve that prison and to secure compensation for its former inmates, and her steely resolve to persist with this campaign despite the threatening behaviour of a former Stasi man, all demonstrate unusual courage.

Both Julia and Frau Paul demonstrate that resilience takes time to develop. Neither woman appears at all strong during Anna's first meetings with them. But upon Anna's return three years later, both are moving on. Resilience is demonstrably a capacity even the most damaged victims have, and one which surfaces in time to carry them out of victimhood and into new life as survivors.

Funder is also interested in the resilience of Stasi personnel, of the men who were involved in inflicting horrors on their own compatriots. As Anna states during her meeting with Koch, she is not interested in what motivated people to join the Ministry, but in 'the process of dealing with that decision now that it is all over' (p.157). There is no single answer. Herr Winz and Herr Bock, still firmly attached to Stasi thought and habit, clearly have no conscious difficulty in dealing with their decisions. The pitiful way in which each is consumed by their commitment to the Firm, demonstrated in Herr Winz's ridiculous faith in a second coming of socialism and in Herr Bock's impotent attempt to threaten Anna, shows an incapacity to move forward, a lack of resilience that Anna finds contemptible. However, contrasting their state to that of the dignified Herr Bohnsack, a man who was prepared to own up to his crimes and to recognise their human toll, shows that acknowledging the faults of the Stasi asks an exacting price. Herr Bohnsack tries to move on, but is lonely and isolated. *Stasiland*'s insiders do not move into the promising, hopeful futures that their victims look set to enjoy.

Key point

Anna's project to portray the legacy of the Stasi's operations is validated by one of the regime's most representative victims: Julia. Julia declares that a regime like the GDR can only be understood through the telling of ordinary stories. She also notes that these stories celebrate survivors, rather than commemorate victims. 'You have to look,' she says, 'at how normal people manage with such things in their pasts' (p.144). Understanding the regime comes through understanding resilience.

Memory and forgetting

Key quotes

'[Y]ou cannot destroy your past, nor what it does to you. It's not ever, really, over.' (p.117)

'Memory, like so much else, is unreliable. Not only for what it hides and what it alters, but also what it reveals.' (p.216)

An undercurrent of disquiet about how quickly things are forgotten runs throughout *Stasiland*. The text asks whether it is healthier to remember or forget through its depiction of characters who variously refuse to remember or refuse to forget. Funder, however, clearly values remembering over forgetting. *Stasiland*, in its compelling depiction of the Stasi and its legacy, is a project 'against forgetting' (p.147).

Memory is both personal and collective

Stasiland's focus on personal stories means that characters share personal memories, and the resultant text becomes a kind of collective biography that testifies to a lost past. Different characters have differing attitudes toward their personal histories. There are characters, like Klaus, who want to forget; those, like Frau Paul, who cannot; and those, including Miriam with her pursuit of Charlie's case, Herr Winz with his research for the *Insiderkomitee* and Koch with his expansive Wall Archive, who refuse to forget. Irrespective of their willingness to remember, each character demonstrates that memory is inherently unreliable because each uses some kind of prop to order, collect or preserve their memories. Klaus keeps copies of his Stasi file on his bookshelf. Frau Paul has her 'short biographical note' (p.205). Julia's shoebox of love letters is an 'aide memoire' (p.117). Herr Winz has his theses, Herr Christian his itinerary of sites, Miriam her box of letters, photographs and poems, and Koch his deep cardboard box of plastic-wrapped evidence. Personal memory is often hinged to a souvenir or artefact that helps make memory tangible.

Collective memory in *Stasiland* also uses physical objects to ground history. There are innumerable museums and memorials in the text. The former Stasi headquarters in Lichtenberg, for example, became a museum only months after the Wall fell. People visit it to see how the Firm operated, to learn about the regime's demise and 'to read their unauthorised biographies' (p.56). The preservation of these biographies – the dossiers of information the Stasi collected on individuals – represents an act of deliberate collective remembering in *Stasiland*. After months of debate about what to do with the Stasi's capacious records, the government of the newly unified Germany created the Stasi File Authority to preserve the files and the people's access to them. Anna's summation of this as a 'brave' and 'conscientious' act (p.71), together with the text's focus on reconstructing personal stories, demonstrates Funder's belief that history, even painful history, should be remembered and preserved.

Memory is political

Stasiland documents a country coming to terms with a difficult and shameful history. In detailing how Germany commemorates its past, Funder demonstrates that collective memory is a highly political domain, a sphere where divergent views compete for the power to determine what is remembered and what is forgotten. The community indecision about what to do with contentious historical sites, such as the Palast der Republik and Hitler's bunker, illustrates the weighty implications of remembering. To preserve a site can imply approval of the activities conducted therein. To demolish it implies denial. Inaction – fencing off the Palast der Republik and reburying Hitler's bunker – seems the least offensive solution, and Anna's Berlin is littered with would-be memorials that show reluctance to engage in the politics of memory: the crumbling Wall, the empty Hohenschönhausen, Koch's guard tower. Scheller's refusal to allow Anna to research Ossis' stories because of the local audience's disinterest similarly indicates a reluctance to remember, a belief that the past is better left untouched. That this particular conversation spurred Anna to meet Miriam and to begin the investigative research that would result in *Stasiland* clearly illustrates that Funder does not subscribe to such a view. She believes things must be remembered because to forget, or simply to ignore the past, is to run the 'risk of doing it all again' (p.51).

This does not mean, however, that Funder views all acts of remembering as equally valid and valuable. Anna is greatly troubled by Leipzig's new museum, which she derides as a 'federally funded effort' to put history 'behind glass' (p.270), and by Berlin's new museum with its pristine reconstruction Wall, which she disparages as 'history, airbrushed for effect' (p.256). Leipzig's new museum features many of the same characters as *Stasiland*, including von Schnitzler, Klaus and Frau Paul. However, without the personal recollections and explanations to make them real, the museum makes the past look 'tawdry' and 'safe' (p.271), a tendency that outrages Anna because it denies the real human impact of this very recent past.

Memory is malleable

One reason for history's being so political is that memory is malleable; that is, it is subject to being distorted or edited, both wilfully and unconsciously. It is this quality of memory that makes Funder so insistent that history be preserved.

There are innumerable examples of wilful forgetting in *Stasiland*, acts that allow people to overwrite and reconstruct the past. Anna observes this in her local neighbourhood, where streets are renamed to deny the area's socialist past (p.52), and in the tricks of language that remove the word 'Führer', the name Hitler adopted for himself, from common conversation (p.104). The extraordinary lengths Stasi personnel went to in order to destroy evidence as revolution swept East Germany also signify a purposeful erasure of memory. Some 15,000 sacks of ruined 'files, index cards, photos and unwound tapes and film' (p.263) were created in the Stasi's frenzied attempt to cover its tracks. Hundreds of shredders were burnt out in the process, leaving men to tear documents with such 'brute strength' that one is described as presumably having 'hardly been able to move his fingers the next day' (p.265).

The problem with this deliberate forgetting, as Funder sees it, is that it allows people to make themselves innocent of their past, both personal and collective. Through these kinds of tricks, East Germans made themselves 'innocent of Nazism' (p.161). Herr Christian claims to be innocent of causing any real damage to the women and children he sent back from the border, just as von Schnitzler can claim the shooting of a would-be escapee was an act of humanity.

Anna realises that 'can't remember' can mean one of two things: the simple inability to recall, to string the memories together, or the choice to avoid thinking about something (p.95). She views the latter as insidious, especially in a place like the former GDR where so much may be disguised and forgotten. Funder's disquiet at the collective preparedness to forget is evident in her wonderment at how quickly the Wall went up and came down again, and at the carefree attitude of Germany's contemporary youth. It is also evident in her frequent observation that the world she is exploring is a lost one, one that will be entirely forgotten in just one generation. Funder believes that the past should be remembered and *Stasiland* may be viewed ultimately as an act of remembrance. As Anna states, 'I'm making portraits of people, East Germans, of whom there will be none left in a generation. And I'm painting a picture of a city on the old fault-line of east and west. This is working against forgetting, and against time' (p.147).

Key point

As a narrator, Anna works in the same way as Herr Koch. Remembering, retelling and preserving are the acts of her work. Her determination to preserve history through collecting and sharing the stories of individuals who lived it suggests Funder believes things need to be remembered, if only to prevent them happening again, because the past is 'not ever, really, over' (p.117).

Trust

Key quotes

> 'Relations between people were conditioned by the fact that one or other of you could be one of *them*. Everyone suspected everyone else, and the mistrust this bred was the foundation of social existence.' (p.28)
>
> 'This society, it was built on lies—lie after lie after lie.' (p.187)

Stasiland reconstructs a world in which ordinary people were subjected to such intense and pervasive scrutiny – even 'activities at kindergartens and dinner parties' were meticulously reported upon (p.200) – that trust in the state and in others became almost impossible. Funder explores the impact of this erosion of trust.

Trust in the state

Citizens of the GDR 'were required to acknowledge an assortment of fictions as fact' (p.96). The Stasi used a myriad of physical, political and psychological facades to sustain and support the regime. Buildings painted just halfway up so that they looked presentable to Honecker observing from the back seat of his limousine (p.187), the swathes of 'pale orange gaps' on Anna's maps that obscure Stasi buildings and operations (p.196) and the prisoner transports disguised as 'linen service vehicles, or refrigerated fish transports, or bakers' vans' (p.225) represent just some of the regime's physical deceits. Political fictions include the myth that East Germans had no responsibility for the Holocaust, that the GDR was a multi-party democracy, that socialism was peace-loving and the Wall an act of humanity, and that prostitution and unemployment didn't exist, a myth laid bare by Julia's frustration when seeking work.

Citizens accepted these fabrications, but not necessarily out of naivety. As Julia states, 'we … felt that our own country was feeding us lies and that our futures depended on seeming to agree with it all' (p.101). But accepting the fictions sometimes came at a terrible cost, a toll Funder illustrates through characterisation. Frau Paul, arguably the text's most damaged character, is a victim of 'GDR-logic' (p.99). Terribly, the Stasi fiction she unwaveringly believes in is the Ministry's construction of her as a criminal. Koch, indoctrinated by the state from an early age and still resolute in his beliefs in the importance of the Wall to prevent trafficking and in America's involvement in trying to starve out citizens of the GDR, demonstrably also subscribes to the state's official fictions.

However, Koch and the sharp-minded Julia also demonstrate what became of faithful citizens whose trust in the state was betrayed. Both are imprisoned by their past – Koch having shifted his near-maniacal faith in the GDR to the Wall, and Julia 'unable to go forward into her own future' (p.95), unable to trust and imagining aggressors all around her.

Trust in others

In a society governed by surveillance and scrutiny, where the number of informers may have been as high as one for every six and a half people (p.57), it was impossible to trust others. Anna's interactions with several characters show the lasting consequences of this perpetual suspicion and suggest that mistrust was not merely 'the foundation of social existence' in the former GDR (p.28), but that it continues in the present.

Herr Winz and Herr Bock, both devoted Stasi men well versed in spying and in coercing the unofficial collaborators who made the Stasi's reach so incredibly expansive, are reluctant to trust Anna. Herr Winz insists on meeting in a covert manner, disguising himself as a westerner, summoning her to a 'neutral place' (p.81) and seeing her identity card. Herr Bock insists that she not use his name in the interview or in her book. These hoops through which Anna is made to jump are more than the mere 'spy play-acting' she dismisses them as (p.85). Rather, these actions show a deep-seated mistrust, something both men have been professional and personally schooled in because of their work with the Stasi.

Experiences with the Stasi and the culture of suspicion it perpetrated also govern Anna's interactions with the Ministry's victims. Julia outright denies having a story of the Stasi to tell, then, with endless coaxing from Anna, reluctantly shares it in piecemeal fashion over a period of weeks. Although a friend of Anna's, Klaus, too, is hesitant to tell his story about the Stasi and obliges only after the pair 'crack open more cans' and the conversation is smoothed by the effects of beer (p.185). The mistrust that each of these characters shows is reinforced by the anonymity of people Anna encounters on the streets and trains of Berlin, people whom she observes closely, but who rarely acknowledge her presence, let alone engage with her. The text's structure also intensifies the undercurrent of alienation left in the wake of the Stasi's destruction of community trust. No two characters' stories interrelate in *Stasiland*. Every character is isolated, reflective of the fractured society Anna observes.

Trust in one's own capabilities

To survive the Stasi's privations and to demonstrate the resilience that Funder celebrates in the text, people needed extraordinary faith in their own abilities. Different characters show differing degrees of faith in their capabilities. Miriam, for example, perhaps fuelled by youthful exuberance and self-belief, had no doubt about her capacity to escape. Looking back, she is impressed and bemused by her fortitude, but as a sixteen-year-old she had no apprehension about scaling the Wall's many accretions. The same boldness carries her through her interrogation and through her persistent investigation of Charlie's case.

Stasi insiders also readily demonstrate this attribute. Von Schnitzler has no doubt about his own authority, or about his forecast of the dangers ahead in capitalist Germany. He demonstrates absolute conviction in his own beliefs, then and now. Herr Winz and Herr Bock enjoy the same certainty, as does Herr Christian, who sees no need to defend his harsh treatment of would-be escapees.

The damage the Stasi could do to a person's self-belief is presented as one of the most damning aspects of its activities. Talented linguist and straight-A student Julia can commit only to part-time study and to casual jobs that fall sadly short of her potential. The combination of her garrulous manner and her inability to trust also indicates a disappointment of her natural talents: she simply cannot make the friends she needs to. Frau Paul, conversely, maintains conviction in her own capabilities, despite having been irreparably wounded by the Stasi. She refused the Stasi's deal without hesitation, utterly convinced that she could not choose her son over her conscience. However, Anna questions the soundness of that conviction. The 'lonely, teary guilt-wracked wreck' (p.221) she interviews does not look like a woman who can trust her own capabilities. In fact, Anna concludes that Frau Paul has drastically 'overestimated her own strength' (p.221). Through Frau Paul, Funder shows that in a society built on lies and suspicion, trust – even in oneself – can easily be misplaced.

Privacy and autonomy

Key quotes

'it's the total surveillance that damaged me the worst' (p.113)

'They lived with a distinct sense … of what could be said outside the home (very little) and what could be discussed in it (most things).' (p.95)

By cataloguing the damages the Stasi inflicted on ordinary people – its targets as well as its own employees – Funder demonstrates that private space, both physical and psychological, is important to emotional health. Privacy is a key facet of autonomy, a person's capacity to govern their own life. When an individual's autonomy is denied, the damage is severe and long lasting.

Miriam's incarceration in Hoheneck prison, where inmates were referred to only by their 'Juvenile Prisoner Number' and forced to ask permission for every small act, leaves her with many 'strange little tics' (p.32). She cannot keep appointments, cuts herself out of her own wedding photos and, suffering from extreme claustrophobia, can only live in spacious, top-storey apartments with views that enable her to 'see anyone coming' (p.14). Julia exhibits similar tendencies, particularly in her inability to submit to the authority of appointments or clocks or regular employment and study. Both women also overreact to perceived aggression. Julia imagines threat from almost every man she encounters. Miriam has 'an automatic flight reaction' that saw her flee her husband whenever he made unexpected movements (p.33). And both are fiercely protective of their privacy, of the small space in their lives that they can control, as demonstrated by their reluctance to respond to Anna's many phone calls and attempts to engage. Julia explains that this reticence arises from a terrible knowledge both characters have. 'I *know*,' remarks Julia, 'how far people will transgress over your boundaries—until you have no private sphere left at all' (p.113).

People survived the Stasi's incursions into their private space by 'sheltering their secret inner lives' in an attempt to 'keep something of themselves from the authorities' (p.96). Effectively, citizens prepared and perpetuated their own facades, appearing outwardly conformist, but maintaining independence of thought in private. The consequences of this fine balance could be tragic. Koch's outwardly conformist father, for example, raised him as 'a poster boy for the new regime' (p.165). Only as an adult did Koch learn that his father was coerced into teaching socialist ideology to schoolchildren under threat of deportation to a Russian prison camp. The knowledge that he had been 'brought up ... as a paragon of a regime [his parents] did not believe in' (p.173) was painful for Koch, and had disastrous implications, causing him to leave the Stasi and costing him his marriage. Julia's father Dieter is another character irreparably damaged by 'Living for so long in a relation of unspoken hostility but outward compliance' (p.96). His years of being ridiculed in Party meetings for wanting to improve socialism left him clinically depressed.

People could hold different private views, but in a world that demanded outward commitment and compliance, the cost of holding those views was high. That this turns otherwise complacent citizens into dissidents or wrecks proves that the state was not 'the good father state' (p.114) faithful citizens believed in, and repudiates Professor Mushroom's naive argument that 'if you didn't buck the system, then it wouldn't harm you' (p.252).

DIFFERENT INTERPRETATIONS

Different interpretations arise from different responses to a text. Over time, a text will give rise to a wide range of responses from its readers, who may come from various social or cultural groups and live in very different places and historical periods. These responses can be published in newspapers, journals and books, both in print and online, by critics and reviewers. They can also be expressed in discussions among readers in the media, classrooms, book groups and so on. While there is no single correct reading or interpretation of a text, it is important to understand that an interpretation is more than a personal opinion – it is the justification of a point of view on the text. To present an interpretation of a text based on your point of view you must use a logical argument and support it with relevant evidence from the text.

Critical viewpoints

Given that it was the 2004 winner of the world's biggest prize for nonfiction and a nominee for numerous Australian and international literary prizes, it is no surprise that critical praise abounds for *Stasiland*. Reviewers applaud the quality, detail and vividness of Funder's prose and the convincing, engaging characters and settings she creates through that language. Jonathan Heawood, for example, credits the 'quality of Funder's prose', which he describes as 'lyrical, bitter, funny and sad' all at once, with making the text 'engaging and important' (Heawood 2004). Funder's employment of an unusual genre – variously described as investigative analysis, reportage, memoir and literary journalism – has also been extolled by critics. The Samuel Johnson Prize's judging committee particularly praised this aspect of *Stasiland*, stating that the book stretched the boundaries of nonfiction writing in an exciting and exemplary way, and that the resultant text constituted 'a fresh and highly original close-up of what happens to people' in a totalitarian state (Josephi & Müller 2009, p.67).

Most critics, however, applaud Funder's text because of the importance of the story she tells. *Stasiland* communicates something of the enormity of the Stasi's legacy and opens up the East German world to outsiders, giving the regime's victims a voice and an identity in doing so. This is seen as an important act of remembering and commemorating, but also as an act of warning. As one reviewer comments, 'The former GDR may be out of the news these days, but Funder's fully humanized portrait of the Stasi's tentacles reads like a warning of totalitarian futures to come' (Kirkus 2003).

Critics are divided on the issue of Funder's status as a foreigner writing about and passing judgement upon a world she never knew. Funder is a westerner writing for a predominantly western audience. It is therefore understandable that critics who come from her own milieu – the Australian and British reviewers and literati who can only view the former GDR from a position remote in both place and time – value Funder's analysis. Such critics consider Funder's foreign perspective to be helpful. Alison Lewis (2002), for example, claims that Funder is bewildered by the former East Germany and that her resultant 'wonderment' enables her to pen 'an intelligent and compassionate engagement with the country and its history'. Elena Lappin (2003) goes further, suggesting that Funder's view from the outside enables her to ask 'all the questions East (and West) Germans should be asking themselves', questions Germans seem reluctant to address from within.

For some, Funder's position as a foreigner imparts clarity. For others, it is a status that encourages the author to pass moral judgement upon something she fails to actually understand. The book was published in Germany in 2004 by an independent publisher, having been rejected by twenty-three publishers; touring the country to promote the book, Funder was scathingly attacked by angry locals who took umbrage at her project. At a book reading held at Runde Ecke, Funder recalls a woman sitting in the back row who 'stood up, cleared her throat, and shouted, "Who gave you the right to write about us?"' (Funder 2004). This bold question encapsulates the angry opposition to Funder's decision to write about a world she barely knows.

Other critics do not question Funder's right to write about the former GDR so much as they question the judgements she makes – and the world she constructs – in so doing. Melbourne University academic Gert Reifarth grew up in East Germany. Asked by a colleague what he made of Funder's text, Reifarth replied 'I never lived in Stasiland' (Reifarth 2007, p.167). It is a country he does not recognise from his own lived experience. He claims that Funder's text describes only the 'black part' of the GDR, and worries that *Stasiland* therefore provides western readers with a misrepresentation of life there prior to 1989. Reifarth describes his experience as '70% grey', where grey represents the regime's reasonably neutral aspects: the overt ideology, the bland and unimaginative architecture and the consistent lies about the country's economic performance. The regime, Reifarth argues, offered some genuine good – a low crime rate, free healthcare and free, high quality, universal education – and these positive features, which he dubs 'white', comprised 20% of his experience, leaving only 10% for the 'black' characteristics that Funder makes the focus of her book.

Two interpretations

Any text is open to contrasting, yet equally valid, interpretations. Here are two possible interpretations of *Stasiland*.

Reading 1

***Stasiland* gives an inaccurate impression of life in the former GDR because its narrator is subjective and unreliable.**

In employing the genre of literary journalism, Funder dismisses the objective, reliable narrative stance of traditional historiography, and instead introduces a first-person narrator to represent the author on the page. This technique inarguably renders the narrative compelling, but it clouds the author's ability to present an objective picture of how life was really lived in the former East Germany.

Funder's stated project in *Stasiland*, as elucidated in Anna's letter to Miriam (p.246), is to explain one peculiar story. She finds that telling that one story demands the explanation of 'other things' (p.246), including insight from 'people who confronted the regime, as much as those who represented it' (p.71), to develop a balanced perspective. This is an admirable ambition, but one Funder has difficulty delivering due to her narrator's prejudice against the Stasi.

Consider her interview with Herr Winz, an episode indisputably coloured by Funder's preconceived ideas about the Ministry. Winz agrees to meet because he believes Anna is granting him an opportunity to provide 'objective information and analysis' (p.81). But Anna is utterly uninterested in hearing Winz's case, to the point of ridiculing it. She 'flicks' through the thesis Winz provides, is incredulous at his description of the *Insiderkomitee* and never reads the copy of the Communist Manifesto he presents to her. Anna is polite and obliging in the meeting, but her narration makes her dismissive stance plain. Her ungenerous characterisation of Winz as an 'underconfident' and 'unconvincing' blusterer (p.85) indicates that she has no interest in hearing his side of history. Herr Bock is described in the same diminishing way as a decrepit man with 'thick square glasses that give him underwater eyes' (p.196) and feet in socks and sandals that dangle helplessly above the floor (p.198). Anna may declare an interest in getting 'perspective', but her encounters with Stasi men show that she refuses to change her convictions about the Stasi.

Anna is similarly dismissive of the regime's positive aspects. Even though many of her favoured characters – Julia and Frau Paul, for example – have no issues with the state until they end up, justly or otherwise, on the wrong side of the law, Anna is reluctant to permit any record of the GDR's advantages. Her only documentation of the regime's benefits is given through the ridiculous Professor Mushroom who laments the loss of security and stability guaranteed in the GDR, a lamentation voiced by a character so pathetic that the reader is not inclined to take his nostalgia seriously.

The characters who are not undermined by slighting characterisation, and whose evidence is recorded without qualification, are those that Funder perceives as 'victims'. There are more chapters – containing far more sympathetic portraits – devoted to the stories of Miriam, Julia and Frau Paul than there are granted to those of Stasi men, and so the text's very structure suggests a prejudicial attitude to the Stasi. The structure further implies that every East German citizen has a story about the Stasi, an impression compounded by Anna's sharing of the stories of characters such as Julia and Klaus, who at first deny having any stories to tell.

Funder's analysis is inaccurate and misleading. This is no fault of her writing, which is always lucid and engaging, but an inescapable flaw of the mode she employs to construct this history. The inevitably subjective first-person narrator leaves Funder utterly unable to consider history from both sides.

Reading 2

The subjectivity of *Stasiland*'s narrator is important to conveying a convincing and comprehensible impression of life in the former GDR.

Of all the creative elements that Funder uses in her historical analysis of a lost time and place in *Stasiland*, her use of a subjective narrator is the most important. The horrors the GDR perpetrated against its own people through the Ministry of State Security are, to most readers, unimaginable. Through Anna, her sympathetic first-person narrator, Funder enables us not only to imagine, but also to be outraged and compassionate.

As a curious and naive foreigner visiting Berlin, Anna's perspective mirrors that of the typical western reader. She introduces us to the alien landscapes she visits – the 'cold grey buildings set in an expanse of gravel' (p.122) and buildings decorated in 'that particular fifties yellowy-green colour, nuclear mustard' (p.72) – with descriptions that vividly communicate her wonderment to the reader. She also acts as a tour guide, furnishing detailed historical information about the regime, its heroes and its demise as she visits key sites. For example, Anna outlines, with the intense interest of a tourist, the biography of Mielke when she visits his office at Stasi HQ (pp.57–9) and the construction of the Berlin Wall when she visits Hagen Koch's Wall Archive (pp.170–1). The accounts of these visits are more than simply descriptions of Anna's personal meanderings. They are an opportunity for Funder to present history in context, a technique that helps the reader make sense of complicated and strange issues.

Funder's subjective narrator also allows the reader to engage emotionally with the text's characters. *Stasiland* presents compelling portraits of victims, people the reader comes to care about as much as Anna does because we see them through her eyes. We are incredulous and outraged when Julia recounts failing the university's political exam (p.102). We empathise with Frau Paul's tragic tale and her 'spasm of pain' (p.221). We are impressed by Miriam's strength as she walks away 'straightbacked into the sunlight' (p.281). Anna's emotional connections with these characters enable the reader to identify with people who have endured unimaginable experiences. Horror is not objective. It can only be communicated by the author's appeal to the reader's emotions, something Funder achieves through her use of a highly subjective narrator.

Anna's nervous fear during her meetings with Stasi men also conveys some of the regime's horror. Herr Bock's quiet menace in the dark flat (p.203), Herr Christian's driving Anna along muddy tracks (p.151) to barren places (p.154) and Herr Winz's demand to see Anna's 'identity card' (p.82) are all moments of palpable disquiet. Anna's trepidation convincingly conveys the power that these men enjoyed in their former roles, and communicates something of the latent fear and suspicion that abounded in the former GDR.

Traditional historiography prides itself on its objectivity. But *Stasiland* does not pretend to be historiography, traditional or otherwise. Nor does Funder set out to be objective. Her project, as Anna explains in a letter to Miriam (p.246), is to tell Miriam's story and to explain what made that woman's tragic story possible. Her project is a compassionate, empathetic one, warranting an entirely subjective approach. This approach is also consistent with Funder's key premise that 'history is made of personal stories' (p.13) and her belief that atrocities should be remembered so that they are not repeated. This makes *Stasiland* a powerful text, one that both remembers and warns. That impact is only possible because the reader has an emotional connection with the narrator, which Funder guarantees by using the subjective Anna to tell the story.

QUESTIONS & ANSWERS

This section focuses on your own analytical writing on the text, and gives you strategies for producing high quality responses in your coursework and exam essays.

Essay writing – an overview

An essay on a literary work is a formal and serious piece of writing that presents your point of view on the text, usually in response to a given essay topic. Your 'point of view' in an essay is your interpretation of the meaning of the text's language, structure, characters, situations and events, supported by detailed analysis of textual evidence.

Analyse – don't summarise

In your essays it is important to avoid simply summarising what happens in a text.

- A **summary** is a description or paraphrase (retelling in different words) of the characters and events. For example: 'Macbeth has a horrifying vision of a dagger dripping with blood before he goes to murder King Duncan.'
- An **analysis** is an explanation of the real meaning or significance that lies 'beneath' the text's words (and images, for a film). For example: 'Macbeth's vision of a bloody dagger shows how deeply uneasy he is about the violent act he is contemplating – as well as his sense that supernatural forces are impelling him to act.'

A limited amount of summary is sometimes necessary to let your reader know which part of the text you wish to discuss. However, always keep this to a minimum and follow it immediately with your analysis of what this part of the text is really telling us.

Plan your essay

Carefully plan your essay so that you have a clear idea of what you are going to say. The plan ensures that your ideas flow logically, that your argument remains consistent and that you stay on the topic. An essay plan should be a list of **brief dot points** – no more than half a page.

- Include your central argument or main contention – a concise statement (usually in a single sentence) of your overall response to the topic. See 'Analysing a sample topic' for guidelines on how to formulate a main contention.
- Write three or four dot points for each paragraph indicating the main idea and evidence/examples from the text. Note that in your essay you will need to *expand* on these points and *analyse* the evidence.

Structure your essay

An essay is a complete, self-contained piece of writing. It has a clear beginning (the introduction), middle (several body paragraphs) and end (the last paragraph or conclusion). It must also have a central argument that runs throughout, linking each paragraph to form a coherent whole.

See examples of introductions and conclusions in the 'Analysing a sample topic' and 'Sample answer' sections.

The introduction establishes your overall response to the topic. It includes your main contention and outlines the main evidence you will refer to in the course of the essay. Write your introduction *after* you have done a plan and *before* you write the rest of the essay.

The body paragraphs argue your case – they present evidence from the text and explain how this evidence supports your argument. Each body paragraph needs:

- a strong **topic sentence** (usually the first sentence) that states the main point being made in the paragraph
- **evidence** from the text, including some brief quotations

- **analysis** of the textual evidence explaining its significance and **explanation** of how it supports your argument
- **links back to the topic** in one or more statements, usually towards the end of the paragraph.

Connect the body paragraphs so that your discussion flows smoothly. Use some linking words and phrases like 'similarly' and 'on the other hand', though don't start every paragraph like this. Another strategy is to use a significant word from the last sentence of one paragraph in the first sentence of the next.

Use key terms from the topic – or synonyms for them – throughout, so the relevance of your discussion to the topic is always clear.

The conclusion ties everything together and finishes the essay. It includes strong statements that emphasise your central argument and provide a clear response to the topic.

Avoid simply restating the points made earlier in the essay – this will end on a very flat note and imply that you have run out of ideas and vocabulary. The conclusion is meant to be a logical extension of what you have written, not just a repetition or summary. Writing an effective conclusion can be a challenge. Try using these tips:

- Start by linking back to the final sentence of the second-last paragraph – this helps your writing to 'flow', rather than just leaping back to your main contention straight away.
- Use synonyms and expressions with equivalent meanings to vary your vocabulary. This allows you to reinforce your line of argument without being repetitive.
- When planning your essay, think of one or two broad statements or observations about the text's wider meaning. These should be related to the topic and your overall argument. Keep them for the conclusion, since they will give you something 'new' to say but still follow logically from your discussion. The introduction will be focused on the topic, but the conclusion can present a wider view of the text.

Essay topics

1. 'Anna is not an objective observer, but this is not a problem. Her subjectivity enhances the impact of *Stasiland*.' Discuss narrative point of view in *Stasiland*.
2. 'Frau Paul is the most damaged character in the text.' Discuss.
3. "I was disappointed in the state. I realised … that it wasn't really the good father state you have in the back of your mind." How do different characters demonstrate the legacy of broken trust?
4. "Suddenly the landscape seems crowded with victims." Are *Stasiland*'s major characters victims?
5. 'Memory is often less about the truth than about what we want the truth to be.' What is the relationship between truth and memory in *Stasiland*?
6. 'Heroes achieve something. *Stasiland*'s key characters cannot be called "heroes" because they don't undermine or destroy the system they resist.' Discuss.
7. In an interview, Funder stated that 'The fundamental thing about writing a novel is to create a believable world and then to have people in it living believable emotional lives.' How does the author create a believable world and believable characters in *Stasiland*?
8. 'The key themes and ideas of *Stasiland* are developed as much by the structure of the text as they are by description and dialogue.' Discuss.
9. 'Courage is resistance to fear, not absence of fear.' Discuss the different kinds of courage demonstrated by the characters in *Stasiland*.
10. 'This text demonstrates that fact is sometimes stranger than fiction.' Discuss.

Vocabulary for writing on *Stasiland*

Literary journalism: A form of nonfiction that combines factual reporting with narrative techniques traditionally associated with fiction.

Objective: Not influenced by personal feelings or opinions in considering and representing facts.

Subjective: Based on or influenced by personal feelings, tastes or opinions.

Analysing a sample topic

In an interview, Funder stated that 'The fundamental thing about writing a novel is to create a believable world and then to have people in it living believable emotional lives.' How does the author create a believable world and believable characters in *Stasiland*?

- Begin by identifying the key words in the question. You might like to underline them. This will help you clarify what the question is really asking. Here, you would probably identify 'believable world', 'believable characters' and 'how' as the key words.
- Spend a few moments considering what these words mean. It is helpful to list some definitions, either your own or those offered by the text or other sources. List some synonyms for each of the key words to help you think about the topic more broadly and to help you vary your vocabulary in your response. Be sure to look up any words that you are not familiar with. This step is all about clarifying the question, so make sure you are very clear about what you are being asked.
- Look for different elements to the question. Is there more than one aspect that needs to be addressed? If a question has multiple elements, a strong answer will need to consider all aspects and examine the tensions among them.

- Think about what the question assumes. Does Funder create a believable world? Are the characters believable? Are both aspects equally convincing, or is one aspect more so than the other? Again, a strong answer must consider all the underlying assumptions of a question.
- Form your own opinion about the statement. Do you agree or disagree? Remember, you are not required simply to agree with the statement. You need to form your own contention and develop a convincing argument using evidence from your reading of the text.
- Note examples from the text that support your opinion, as your response requires textual evidence. Jot down notes about *why* you agree or disagree, too.
- All this will help you form your own contention, which you will argue in your response. A good way to form your contention is to modify the statement so that it reflects your ideas. Your modified statement should encapsulate the argument you intend to make and will guide you as you write. A response to this question might contend that 'Funder creates equally realistic characters and settings in *Stasiland* through descriptive and figurative language, attention to detail, clever structuring and a skilfully managed narrative point of view.'

Sample introduction

Funder re-creates a lost world in *Stasiland*, one from which many contemporary readers are removed by both time and place. For such readers to comprehend the Stasi's impact, the text's settings and characters must be believable. Funder achieves this through her use of highly descriptive and figurative language, her precise attention to detail, the structure of the text and her skilful management of a complex narrative point of view. Through these techniques, Funder brings the imaginative features of fiction writing to a nonfiction text and, in so doing, creates an absorbing and compelling narrative world that credibly documents the horrors the Stasi inflicted upon its own people.

Body paragraph outline

Funder's highly descriptive and frequently figurative language paints vivid portraits of people and places so that the reader can identify with an otherwise alien world.

- The use of simile and metaphor in descriptions (Miriam's haircut, pp.14–15; Herr Christian's smile, p.149; Herr Winz, p.81) enables the reader to visualise distinct characters and helps to convey complex emotions so that the reader can empathise (Julia as hermit crab, p.90; Miriam as a fairytale maiden, p.228; Herr Bohnsack, p.243).
- Descriptive language convincingly conveys foreign and terrifying settings (long corridors and multi-purpose rooms, pp.123–4; Mielke's office, pp.72–3; torture devices, pp.226–7).

The precision of Funder's language and her attention to detail enable her to construct thoroughly convincing characters and settings.

- The descriptions of streets (p.72, p.122), Hohenschönhausen (p.224, p.226), the station (pp.1–2) and the weather (p.214) enable the reader to clearly visualise Berlin.
- Detailed observations of both major and minor characters render them realistic and believable (von Schnitzler, p.129; Frau Paul and house, p.205; punks and drunks, pp.248–52).

The structure of the text focuses attention on individuals in turn, enabling the reader to come to know the characters in depth.

- Each character has their own chapter, except those who have several (Miriam, Julia, Frau Paul, Koch). This allows Funder narrative space to provide detail and to convey emotional impact, and also absorbs the reader in a personal narrative.
- Settings are given meaning and context and thereby rendered realistic (Fall of the Wall at Stasi HQ, pp.61–6; construction of the Wall and meeting Koch, p.171; Mielke's background at Stasi HQ, pp.57–9).

The narrative point of view guides the reader through unfamiliar terrain and the reader's understanding of this world grows as Anna's own understanding does.

- Anna is a foreigner/stranger – everything is new to her as much as to the reader (conversation with Miriam, p.28; swimming pool, pp.145–7; Nuremberg, pp.262–4). We sympathise with certain characters and situations because she takes the reader with her.
- The narrator frequently lets characters speak uninterrupted (Julia, pp.141–5; Koch, pp.158–60; Frau Paul, pp.217–20). This gives characters voice, building full and believable emotional lives for them in the text.

Sample conclusion

Creating a believable world peopled with characters who have full, believable emotional lives might be the foundation of a successful novel, but it is also essential to Funder's nonfictional portrait of a vanished time. Funder brings techniques from fiction – including the use of figurative language, precise detail in characterisation and setting, an asynchronous structure and a first-person narrator – to her history and, through these, develops convincing characters and vivid settings. In doing so, she rescues real people from the injuries inflicted by the Stasi, restoring identity and humanity where the Stasi took it away, and creates a narrative world so memorable that this vanished time cannot be forgotten or denied. *Stasiland* is, consequently, a powerful and restorative act of remembering.

SAMPLE ANSWER

'Frau Paul is the most damaged character in the text.' Discuss.

Frau Paul, 'a lonely, teary guilt-wracked wreck', is a striking example of the damage perpetrated by the Stasi in *Stasiland*. However, to say she is definitively the most wounded is to ignore the many harms illustrated by the text's other characters, and to overlook Frau Paul's strength. *Stasiland*, as an investigation of the many 'kinds of courage' exhibited by people in the GDR, is populated with injured characters from both inside and outside the Stasi. Examining other major characters shows that Frau Paul cannot be singled out as the text's most damaged character.

Frau Paul is inarguably wounded. Fragile and tearful, she cannot talk to Anna without 'holding onto notes on her own life'. She 'loses her thread' and is unable to tell the truth about her own life, as evidenced by her denial of involvement in the smuggling syndicate in which she appears to have been a hero. Perhaps her self-image is the greatest indicator of damage: she sees herself as the Stasi constructed her, as 'a criminal'. Despite these injuries, Frau Paul is also resilient, and to cast her as the text's most damaged character discounts her obvious strength. She refused the Stasi's deal, choosing her conscience over her son. She takes Anna to Hohenschönhausen – 'the place that broke her' – where she works as a tour guide, and she bravely campaigns for the prison's preservation despite the threatening actions of an ex-Stasi man. She is damaged, but also principled, courageous and 'steely'.

The text's other female characters, Julia and Miriam, are similarly courageous. In fact, their composure – neither cry during their meetings with Anna – make them appear outwardly stronger than Frau Paul, but this belies the damage that so obviously shapes their lives. Julia is incapable of trust, reacts 'strongly to harassment' (real or imagined), and is 'only part-attached to the world'. While Frau Paul works as a dental technician and is active in community groups, Julia is capable only of part-time, temporary work, well below the career her natural abilities promised. She is 'unable to go forward into her own future', resistant to intimacy (conveyed in the simile likening her to a hermit crab 'ready to whisk back into its shell at the slightest sign of contact') and 'regards fixed appointments as intolerable constraints on her freedom'. Miriam similarly regards fixed appointments as 'an unbearable obligation'. She, like Julia and Frau Paul, is imprisoned by her past, and lives her life as an 'epitaph to a life that was', illustrated by her refusal to give up searching for answers about Charlie's death and her inability to have a 'partner in life'. All three women are irreparably damaged in equally devastating and lasting ways.

Stasiland's male characters are not impervious to injury, and the curious behaviour of some challenges the assertion that Frau Paul is the text's most damaged character. Hagen Koch, for example, for all his confidence and exuberance, exhibits the same incapacity to move forward as Julia, Miriam and Frau Paul. Raised as a 'poster boy for the new regime' with a belief in the GDR that bordered on religious faith, Koch lives his life in the shadow of the vanished Wall. His devotion to the state betrayed, he fixates on the Wall, commemorating it in his 'Wall Archive' with a maniacal fervour that renders him incapable of embracing the future. As Anna observes, like Frau Paul, Koch simply will not – cannot – let go. He, too, is consumed and defined by his past, a past created for him by the Stasi.

Other male characters are also imprisoned by the identities forged by the Stasi. Herr Winz, with his disguise, his covert plans and his insistence on seeing Anna's identity card, is a man still playing 'spy games seven years after the fall of the Wall'. Herr Bock similarly insists Anna follow the rigmarole of a Stasi interview, instructing her not to use his name and enjoying his menacing power. Both men refuse to concede the invalidity of their dearly held views and are consequently pitifully out of touch with the world in which they find themselves. The more open Herr Bohnsack fares little better, for all his candidness. He is socially isolated, friendless, 'fallen between two stools'. Though the damage may be less obvious, each of these characters is as irrevocably damaged as Frau Paul.

Torsten, Frau Paul's son, declares that 'there are no people who are whole'. *Stasiland*'s many characters show this to be true. Not one is unscarred. Funder's text is a catalogue of damage that indicts the Stasi, its activities and its methods. To say one character is more or less damaged than another is to miss the full picture expressed by the text's cumulative horrors, a picture that acts as a 'warning from the past' to diminish the 'risk of doing it all again'.

REFERENCES & READING

Text

Funder, Anna 2002, *Stasiland*, Text Publishing, Melbourne.

Other references

Funder, Anna 2004, 'A Stranger in the East', *The Telegraph*, 7 June, www.telegraph.co.uk/culture/books/3618556/A-stranger-in-the-east.html

Heawood, Jonathan 2004, 'In the company of spies', *The Guardian*, 20 June, www.guardian.co.uk/books/2004/jun/20/features.review1

Josephi, Beate & Müller, Christine 2009, 'Differently Drawn Boundaries of the Permissible in German and Australian Literary Journalism', *Literary Journalism Studies*, vol.1, no.1, Spring, pp.67–78.

Kirkus Reviews 2003, 'Stasiland', www.kirkusreviews.com/book-reviews/anna-funder/stasiland/#review

Lappin, Elena 2003, 'Up against the wall', *The Sunday Times*, 8 June, p.43.

Lewis, Alison 2002, 'State Secrets', *The Age*, 11 May, p.8.

Reifarth, Gert 2007, 'Born in the GDR', *Meanjin*, vol.66, no.2, pp.164–171.

Shakespeare, Nicholas 2003, 'What was a wall is now a gulf', *The Telegraph*, www.telegraph.co.uk/culture/books/3596273/What-was-a-wall-is-now-a-gulf.html

Further reading

The Lives of Others 2006, dir. Florian Henckel von Donnersmarck, Wiedemann & Berg Productions. Starring Martina Gedeck, Ulrich Mühe and Sebastian Koch.

Funder, Anna n.d. *Stasiland*, http://annafunder.com/stasiland

Maher, Michael 2006, 'Stasiland', *Foreign Correspondent*, ABC-TV, www.abc.net.au/foreign/content/2006/s1749406.htm